Ask For More

Richard Bellman

Life On Purpose Publishing
WINDSOR, CONNECTICUT

Ask For More

Richard Bellman

All Rights Reserved.
Copyright © 2017 by **Richard Bellman**
Cover Design © 2017 by **JAM Designs**
Edited by **Dr. Angela D. Massey.**

Printed in the United States of America. Except as permitted under the United States Copyright Act of 1976, no part of this book may be reproduced in any form or by any electronic or mechanical means including information storage and retrieval systems—except in the case of brief quotations in articles or reviews—without the prior written permission of its publisher, Life on Purpose Publishing and/or Richard Bellman

All brand names and product names used in this book are trademarks, registered trademarks, or trade names of their respective holders

This publication is designed to provide accurate and authoritative information in regard to the subject matter covered. It is sold with the understanding that neither the publisher nor the author is engaged in rendering legal or other professional services. If legal advice or other expert assistance is required, the services of a competent professional person should be sought.

—From a declaration of principles jointly adopted by a committee of the American Bar Association and a committee of publishers.

A Gap Closer ™ Publication
    A Division of Life On Purpose Publishing
    Windsor, Connecticut

Ask for More/Richard Bellman
ISBN 13: 978-0-9961908-7-9

Dedication:
to My Parents

Contents

Introduction xi

ASK FOR RESPONSIBILITY

1 What Uniform Are You Wearing? 1
2 Start Here: Taking the Initiative 9
3 Take A Risk! 17
4 Now What? Commit to Your Dreams 27
5 What's Your Motivation? 35

ASK FOR INCREASE

6 Engagement and Expectations 47
7 I Think I Can 57
8 Will Power and Self-Discipline 65
9 Procrastination and Other Roadblocks 75
10 Execution, Effort and Excellence 81

ASK FOR CHARACTER

11 Courage 93
12 Faith 103
13 Patience 113
14 Integrity 121
15 Resilience 129

ASK FOR HEALTH

16 Weight 139
17 Exercise 147
18 Sleep 157
19 Companionship and Health 167
20 Mindful Meditation and Health 175

ASK FOR MORE EDUCATION

21 Intelligence and Achievement 187
22 Intelligence and New Learning Can Change the Brain 195
23 Mindset 205
24 Deep Practice 215
25 Coaching 223

ASK FOR SUCCESS

26 The Meaning of Success 233
27 Why We Fail 241
28 Attract Success Into Your Life 249
29 Regrets: What Gets Left Behind 257
30 Gratitude and Success 267

References 275

"Please, sir, I want some more."
"What?" said the master at length, in a faint voice.
"Please, sir," replied Oliver, "I want some more."

– CHARLES DICKENS
OLIVER TWIST

Introduction

Throughout my teaching career, I taught various subjects based on the assigned course books. These books aligned with the curriculum that I was going to teach. I used them to direct the material towards my students in a way that they would learn the subject well enough to pass certification exams to further their career. In writing Ask for More, I wanted to create a guide to achieving one's dreams, a template for the future. I wanted to help my readers unlock their true potential by asking for more of themselves. By asking for more of ourselves, we can reach our true potential and succeed at all of our goals, whatever they might be. By holding ourselves accountable for all of our successes and failures, we can learn from our mistakes and grow mentally and spiritually. All learning is growth, and through Ask for More I wanted to help the reader grow and achieve real success.

I divided the book into six sections: Responsibility, Increase, Character, Health, Education, and Success. I wanted the acronym to spell riches since that is what everyone seemingly wants. Yet, did you know that if you earn $25,000 a year you are in the top 1% of the world's wealthy? True riches and wealth are matters of perspective. In each section, I offer the reader insights and expert information so that he or she can make real executive decisions about the future. If the reader follows some of these steps and suggestions in all six sections of the book, different areas of life will become richer and more meaningful. Asking for more is a process and one that must be practiced with patience.

In the Responsibility section of the book, I discuss the roles that we play in our lives and the various uniforms we wear in our work lives. I discuss accountability for all of our actions and the need to avoid falling victim to events in our lives or laying blame. Through taking the initiative, we can take control of various situations in our lives, whose outcomes we would like to change. By taking calculated risks, we can attempt to change the course of our actions and rise above our mistakes. Through a commitment to our goals, we can make a positive change towards fulfilling our goals. Lastly, through understanding our motivation, that is our reason for pursuing various goals in our lives, we can better plot our best course of action to suit that motivation. Find your mountain, and you will find your motivation or your reason to get started.

In the Increase section of the book, I describe strategies that will help you improve on yourself and allow you to get even closer to your goals and objectives. Most people still believe that people with high salaries caught some lucky break or have special connections in the company. High salaries are paid to individuals who are engaged in their work and love what they do. If employees are engaged at work, they will become more productive and happy with their work. The more we expect of ourselves, the greater our productivity will be. Considering your life's purpose is crucial to increasing our expectations on the road to success.

I will show examples of innovators who dared to be different in their thinking and pursue their passions regardless of the cost or time it took. They did whatever it took to achieve success. In this section, I also discuss willpower and self-discipline and how it can be applied to goals such as weight loss, reducing stress and dieting. Many people tend to procrastinate and put other roadblocks in their way. These types of procrastinators will be introduced in this section as well along with plans to execute your dreams into action. Many people have great ideas, but never put their ideas into physical or concrete action.

In the Character section of the book, I delve into character traits that we need to pursue anything in life, or any goal or dream. Aren't there always those people who will tell us that "it'll never work" and "here's why." People always want to give us their feedback, and it's usually negative. It takes courage to live your dream and stand up to people who will challenge you. It will take faith to stand up to your self-limiting beliefs and negative self-talk. At times we could be our own worst enemies. Success takes time. Your goals require your patience and perseverance so that you don't give up too soon. Integrity and especially self-integrity is crucial to achieving your goals. So often we lie to ourselves when we blame time, people and other circumstances for our lack of success. Finally, resilience is important to have while working towards our dreams. Resilience will keep you strong during times of struggle and allow you to bounce back and thrive.

Without good health, you can never really achieve anything of lasting value, or at the very least get to enjoy it and share it with those close to you and the people you want to help with your product or services. Your health and vitality will allow you to put forth a consistent effort to reach your goals. In the Health section of the book, I included a chapter on weight. Weight control is so important in preventing other diseases such as heart disease and stroke. Exercise is crucial to physical and mental health and has been proven to stimulate good moods and positive attitudes. Modern technology has made us lazy and inactive. The average American looks at screens for 7 hours every day. Over 80% of Americans don't get the recommended 150 minutes of exercise every week. Rest and proper sleep are also vital to our overall health and productivity. Proper sleep will prevent stroke, over-eating, anxiety, depression and mood swings. Some companies in the United States will allow you to take a nap if that means you will be a more productive worker. For many years as a bachelor, I thought I could go through life alone, but in the chapter on Companionship and Health, there is strong research that supports companionship, friendship, social bonds and marriage to lead a fulfilling and successful life. Lastly, in Mindful Meditation and Health, I explore the tremendous mental and physical health benefits which can be derived from meditation. You don't have to climb the mountain to ask a guru about life's big questions. You can meditate wherever you find yourself and find yourself through meditating!

As a teacher, it was crucial for me to include an Education section. You might start your goal with a solid why, or a sense of purpose for doing something or achieving a certain goal, but if you don't know how, you'll have a hard time of getting it off the ground. In this section, I also address some key hot-button issues such as the relation of intelligence to achievement and explore Howard Gardner's theory of multiple intelligences and how emotional intelligence relates to an individual's success. Is intelligence fixed or can it be enhanced or improved upon through learning? Yes, sir, you in the front row! Learning can enhance specific skills as we will learn in this section. Not cut out for college? That's what you told yourself, and you have to change your mindset from a fixed mindset to a growth mindset. Also in this section, deliberate practice can improve any skill, and it doesn't have to take 10,000 hours, but a focused and dedicated intention for success at your goal! Find a coach who will give you that extra nudge as in the examples I present in this section such as John Wooden, coach of the UCLA Bruins who also developed the pyramid of success.

In the last section, Success, I bring everything together. In the first chapter of the section, I discuss the meaning of success. Success can mean different things to different people from all over the world. What about a single mom who holds down two jobs to support her sons and saves so that they could go to college? Success is all about what gives you the most meaning in your life. Also in this section, I discuss why we fail. Think about it. We fail because we gave up too early, didn't believe in ourselves enough, didn't persist enough, or something came along; this is why we have to attract success in our lives

ASK FOR MORE

through the Law of Attraction. By affirming that we are already the people we want to be and have the things that we want to have, we are imprinting the subconscious mind to believe it is true. All we have to do is to ask, believe, and receive. If we take massive action towards our goal, then the universe will take notice. I discuss the top five regrets of the dying, and neither of the five includes I wish I had made more money! Live a life true to yourself and follow your dreams now and you have already taken care of the first regret! Lastly, by expressing gratitude for all that you have in life so far, you will attract more abundance and success into your life. By counting your blessings every day for all that you have and expressing your gratitude for the miracle of life and the world and all that is in it, you will attract more of whatever it is you are grateful for! Thank you for taking this journey with me. Ask for more RICHES, and the world will attract those riches to you in ways you had never even imagined!

Richard Bellman
San Pedro, California

Ask For Responsibility

WHAT UNIFORM ARE YOU WEARING?

At the height of the recession in April of 2010, I worked as an AAA Roadside Assistance driver. I had tried to be a "Master of the Universe," coming off a two-year career as a stockbroker and life insurance agent. Since I didn't have a book of business, I wasn't able to ride out the tough times. I tried to build a book of business, but I couldn't convince clients to buy investment products or life insurance contracts when people's homes were being foreclosed on, and they were losing their portfolios. A neighbor who ran a towing company with two of his brothers and had a contract with AAA gave me a job. After two weeks of unpaid training, I operated one of the trucks and got calls from members for emergency gas, lockouts, dead batteries and flat tires.

One night, when the truck was garaged at our apartment, I was with my then six-year-old son who needed me to adjust the seat on his bicycle. I hadn't noticed that he had grown. So, I used my tools to adjust the seat and had him try it out. He rode around the garage a bit, thanked me, and then said, "Dad, I like your uniform." I said, "Michael, the job is brutal. I get 12 to 15 calls a day, and I am out there in the heat working my butt off!" Then he got off his bicycle and said, "I didn't say I want the job, Dad. I said I like the uniform!"

As adults, we know that wearing the uniform represents our responsibility to perform the job that we are tasked to do. Of course, at the time, my son couldn't appreciate how hard it was for me to even get into a mechanic's uniform: blue Dickies, a blue collared shirt with reflective stripes and black steel toe boots. I accepted the responsibility of wearing the uniform and performed all of the duties that came with it. For me, I thought wearing it meant that I had hit rock bottom, that I was a disappointment to myself and my family. But, I think as young as he was, he was really saying, "Dad, thanks for putting on the uniform for us, for taking that responsibility for us, for the family."

When students wear school uniforms, they are reminding themselves when they get up and get ready for school that they are taking the responsibility to adhere to the school's rules and regulations. When police officers wear their uniforms, they are expressing their responsibility to protect and serve the public in their respective communities. When military service men and women are seen wearing their uniforms in supermarkets and airports around the country, they are also expressing their responsibility and commitment to our great country. When workers in the retail and service industry wear their respective uniforms, they are expressing their rank and file to each other and the public at large. What uniform are you wearing right now in life? What responsibilities do you have in your life? What are you committed to? Who have you committed to? Are you living up to your current responsibilities?

When you ask for responsibility, you are forced to take ownership of your responsibilities and whether large or small, commit to following them through to completion. Whenever you take on a new responsibility, you are telling yourself, first and foremost, that you are willing to be fully accountable; that you're ready to take on tasks that you may not have taken on previously. You hold yourself accountable to other people: employers, spouses, and children whenever you ask for responsibility.

If you have ever signed a job application, a marriage contract, or had your name on a baby's birth certificate, you are assuming a new responsibility. You are asking for responsibility and accountability with an unspoken promise that you will fulfill the role and the position to the best of your ability. Always remember that even when the job gets tough, the marriage falters, or the relationship with your children intensifies or falters, you asked for the responsibility. You signed up for it!

By asking for responsibility, you are stepping into the world of choice. You are consciously creating your life and finding your place in the world. Responsibility is the ability to use your free will. It enables you to claim power over yourself and your life. Taking responsibility means acting autonomously without the authorization of others. This state of empowerment makes you fully capable of owning the consequences of the choices you make in your life.

Since the word *responsibility* comes from the Latin response (responsum) which means to answer for, we are responsible when we answer for our actions and our behavior. When life is great, and we receive credit for a positive outcome, we gladly accept our responsibility for the role we played. However, when a negative event happens in our lives, we are wary of taking responsibility for the outcome. How we respond to a negative event will determine the outcome that we desire.

If a negative event occurs in your life, you must first take responsibility for it, analyze how it happened, and then choose a response to change the event for the better to realize your intended outcome. If you got yourself into a problematic situation, you must take responsibility to remove yourself from that situation. Take the time to find out why something happened. It didn't happen to you; it happened because of you and something you did. For example, if you are facing bankruptcy, maybe it's because you used cash advances from your credit cards as extra income for several years. Then, you grew accustomed to the lifestyle that you enjoyed because of the extra income, but couldn't keep up the payments to the banks that loaned you the money. Your decision to use cash advances resulted in your inability to keep up the payments. In essence, you weren't responsible because you couldn't afford to pay them back from your monthly income from your job!

All too often, we play victim to our problems. Victimhood is the opposite of responsibility. We feel like victims when we suffer a loss or harm psychologically or financially. We blame a third party or an outside entity for our problems. When we don't take full responsibility and answer for our feelings, actions, and behavior, we are blaming someone or something else for what has happened to us such as our partner, spouse, boyfriend or girlfriend, the economy, the market or the government.

When we take responsibility for the events in our lives, it drives us to focus on positive change. We are empowered to take action, and we don't need the approval of others to do so. When we choose victimhood, we not only isolate ourselves from others, but all of the anger and feelings of resentment and betrayal largely go unnoticed, since other people cannot be accountable for our lives.

Remember that only you can take control of your life. No matter your age, status, intelligence or education, you can ask for the responsibility to change your life and live your dreams. Throughout the course of this book, I will show you how to do this by first asking for responsibility and then charting the course of the rest of your life.

Changing your life is possible! When you ask for responsibility, you position yourself to experience new opportunities and new endeavors. By using the steps I will share with you in this book, you will be able to:

- Break a lifelong addiction
- Leave a destructive relationship
- Start a new business
- Go back to school or complete your degree

- Get married or get divorced
- Quit a job that doesn't suit you anymore
- Become an entrepreneur

The steps I will outline throughout the course of this book will inspire you to apply the principals to all aspects of your life.

Action Steps

1. Describe an event in your life, positive or negative, for which you took responsibility.
2. Describe an event in your life when you felt like a victim. Who betrayed you? What was the outcome?
3. What new challenges are you facing now? What new responsibilities will you ask for tomorrow, next week, and next month?
4. What are your dreams for the future? For example, is there a book in you? Are you being asked to make a presentation to your staff? Do you have any plans to travel? Are you planning to retire from your job to pursue other interests?
5. Make a list of all of the jobs you have ever had. Were they related in any way? What did you learn about yourself once they were done? Were they all "worthwhile" in terms of your personal growth?
6. Do you feel that you are a responsible friend, spouse, and parent? Do all of these roles carry a set of responsibilities? Are there any that need improvement? If so, why?

2 Start Here: Taking the Initiative

The average American works nearly 34.4 hours per work week. Americans work longer than most people in other developed countries; for example, citizens in Austria work a mere 30.3 hours, while people in Norway work 26.6 hours per week. Also, according to a recent Gallup poll, many adults who work full-time said that they work even more than the reported 34.4 hours, clocking in 47 hours per week. Nearly 4 in 10, or 40% report working 50 or more hours each week.

RICHARD BELLMAN

While Americans work hard compared to other countries around the world, most start watching the clock on Monday morning at 9:00 a.m. and continue until Friday at 5:00 p.m. Even though jobs are still in high demand, many people have been forced out of retirement because of the economic recession. In essence, many workers are just getting by which means that they might not be psychologically invested in their jobs or to the overall success of the company. Many workers do just enough to fulfill the list of duties on the job description. They aren't engaged enough to ask for responsibility or take the initiative necessary to get ahead in their careers and their lives.

If you want real action in your life, you have to ask for more responsibility. Wishing doesn't make it so. The time will never be right for you to achieve your dream. You have to start here. The old work model of working longer hours or working multiple jobs is outdated. To ask for more responsibility means you have to take the initiative. You have to control your life and your destiny!

So, what does taking the initiative mean? When you take the initiative, you show a willingness to get things done and to be responsible. You are willing to take the first steps towards your goal, your product or your mission. When you take the initiative, you recognize that something needs to happen, and you're no longer willing to wait for the right opportunity to make it happen. You create the opportunity. It's better to be ready for an opportunity and not have one than to have an opportunity and not be ready! If you are the kind of person who needs to serve others and serve yourself, then you must take the initiative on your job, in your family, and your relationships.

A person who takes the initiative is willing to get things done on their terms. When you take the initiative, you are looking for solutions that will help your project, your team, and your company. You are proactive about what needs to happen before it happens. By taking the initiative, you dare to think differently. You choose activities that support your passions and your goals.

People who take the initiative take responsibility for their actions. Employers are looking for employees who take the initiative and look to add value to the organization they work for, and thereby help themselves through their actions. Look for ways to take the initiative at work and in your life. At work, you can offer co-workers your assistance and feedback on a project they are working on. You can consult with your boss to see if he needs help with a certain project or ask her for more challenging tasks than you are already handling.

When you take the initiative at work, you always learn first and then do later. If you can't complete an assignment, take a class or find a mentor who can help you.

RICHARD BELLMAN

Taking the initiative means asserting your independence and solving problems on your own. At group meetings speak up and offer your feedback and constructive criticism. Don't be shy to express your views and ideas; they have value and worth. You are showing that you are a strong member of the team unafraid to make contributions to everyone's benefit.

Apply the idea of asking for more responsibility and taking the initiative to all aspects of your life. Sometimes deciding to act, even concerning small decisions, can be a major challenge for some people. At times, there are things that we need to do, but due to procrastinating and blaming, we don't take the initiative. In your intimate relationships, be the one to make certain concessions if it will add to the harmony of the relationship. Be the one to break stalemates or arguments even if the argument was not your fault. Be the first to reach out to loved ones and friends after long absences and preserve the relationship.

Research suggests that 95% of all people who make New Year's resolutions break them by January 15th. We have all done it. We make the resolution because we feel we have to since others around us are making resolutions, especially to lose weight! We are caught up in the spirit of change. We are motivated to act because the calendar is going to change, and we feel that we have to change with it—this is where taking the initiative comes into play. If

ASK FOR MORE

you want to lose weight, taking small initiatives such as eating smaller portions, eating on smaller plates, and eating at least five fruits and vegetables every day go a long way towards achieving your goal of losing weight and keeping your resolution. Taking the initiative can change your life!

If you have dreams and goals that you want to achieve, make a list of all of them and then break them down into smaller goals. You may have plans that you are putting off because of procrastinating. If you benefit from putting off your dreams, then continue to wait. Usually, waiting makes completing your goals harder. If you want to take action on a big goal or a dream, take a small initiative to achieve it.

If you always wanted to act, take some local acting classes. If you want to write a book, purchase an affordable laptop and take a writing class. If you would like to sing, hire a voice coach and build a repertoire of songs that you enjoy and then consider writing your songs. If you want to become a public speaker, join a local Toastmaster's where you can build your skills.

Taking the initiative means being proactive with your life. Change your frame of mind and don't wait for others around you to take action. Initiative means doing the right thing without being told. When it comes to taking the initiative, there are four types of people: Which one are you?

1. People who take the initiative are people who do the right thing without being told. They experience high rewards/high financial gains.
2. People who do the right thing after being told what to do are those who experience average rewards/average financial gains.
3. People who do the right thing after doing the wrong thing and being told what not to do are those who experience low rewards/low financial gains.
4. People who do the wrong thing all the time are people who experience no rewards/no financial gains.

Write down three reasons why taking action towards achieving your goals are important to you. Knowing what you want is empowering! After writing down your reasons to act, you can then break those down into small initiatives that you can accomplish right away. Doing so can help you build the confidence to realize achieving your larger goal, thus getting you that much closer to accomplishing your dream.

ASK FOR MORE

In his book, *The Inward Journey*, Howard Thurman wrote:

> *"The Decision to Act: It is a wondrous thing that a decision to act releases energy in the personality. For days on end, a person may drift along without much energy, having no particular sense of direction, and having no will to change. Then something happens to alter the pattern. It may be something very simple and inconsequential in itself, but it stays awake, it alarms, it disturbs. In a flash, one gets a vivid picture of one's self—and it passes. The result is a decision—a sharp, definitive decision. In the wake of the decision, yes, even as part of the decision itself, energy is released. The act of decision sweeps all before it, and the life of the individual may be changed forever."*

Action Steps

1. After taking the Initiative Quiz, what number are you? Are you ready to change?
2. What initiatives do you plan to take right now, at work, at home, and in your current relationships?
3. Think of a recent event at work or home when taking the initiative averted a crisis. Now think of one in your life. What steps are you prepared to take right now?
4. Try taking small initiatives in your life that affect other people such as practicing small random acts of kindness. Here are a two ideas:
    - Let people in front of you in checkout lines
    - Feed someone who can't afford lunch.
5. How do those initiatives feel?

3 TAKE A RISK

Every initiative involves a certain element of risk. Everything we do involves risk of failure, shame, embarrassment and possible financial loss. On the other hand, taking a risk could eventually lead to recognition, acclaim, high financial rewards, and fame. Many of us like playing it safe. We like the idea of "job security," knowing that if we stay in our lanes and don't break rank or deviate from the norm, we will be okay. Living life in a secure comfort zone when there are no mistakes, no stress and no failures doesn't sound very adventurous, does it? Then why don't we take more risks?

RICHARD BELLMAN

Since by definition, *risk* is "the possibility of danger," it's a wonder why we take any action at all. Our early ancestors had to escape predators, but all we have to do is overcome our fear and our negative self-talk. When we meet someone, there is the risk that the initial attraction could lead to a long-term relationship or complete incompatibility. There is always the risk that marriage could lead to divorce, and it often does, but people still get married every day. Childbirth is a risky process, but babies are being born every day. If we lead sheltered, comfortable lives, we will never be truly fulfilled.

The need for security keeps us from enjoying a truly adventurous, engaging and successful life. When we don't ask for more responsibility in our lives and take the initiative to achieve our goals in the face of risk, we won't grow or adapt to our changing environment. We have to feel challenged to grow, and the only way to do so is to take risks.

When you take a calculated risk, some may see you as unconventional. Taking a risk is scary since you are going to do something that isn't predictable. So, one of the main reasons why we don't take risks is because we don't know the outcome. We like being in control, and when we take risks, we lose some of that control.

By calculating a risk, we are weighing the possible benefits of our actions. We are also considering the negative aspects of taking the risk. The key is not to focus on the potential negative aspects of the risk before we take action because people tend to ruminate and dwell on the possible "what ifs," especially the negative outcomes. Dwelling on the "what ifs" could lead us to freeze up. Our inaction and inability to take the initiatives and the risks attached to them then become our first failure. Of course, the best risk to take is one where the potential upside far outweighs the potential loss. However, taking no action and the associated risk means there's no way to know!

You have to put yourself out there. You have to take a risk and find out. There are so many benefits to risk-taking, but without taking the initiative, there's no way to know what those benefits are.

Benefits of Taking Risks

Most Americans are risk adverse since we are afraid that we won't be able to fully recover whatever we lose when we take a risk. We should realize that not all risk involves loss. Sometimes when we take a risk we are basically taking a chance on ourselves, our talents and abilities. We as a population would not have come this far had it not been for the people who took risks to advance their achievements and make a contribution to the world. Here are some of the benefits of taking risks.

- **Reframe taking a risk as a new opportunity:** Whether it's a career move, promotion, going back to school or being selected to take a business trip, every risk carries with it an opportunity to succeed once you take the initiative and assume the risk.
- **Taking a risk distinguishes you from the crowd:** You are showing others that you are a leader who isn't afraid to take action. Above all, you are proving your self-worth and abilities to yourself.
- **You can learn a great deal about yourself when you take risky initiatives:** You will also find a way to learn the necessary skills to get closer to your goals and objectives.
- **Risk-taking could lead to eventual success:** By taking the initiative and risk, you will move closer to your goal. Celebrate each small initiative and success since they will serve to build momentum as you strive towards your ultimate goal. Success will not fall into your lap. You must chase it, hunt it, and pursue it.
- **You won't ever achieve your dreams by staying in your comfort zone:** Life coach and speaker Tony Robbins once said. "If you keep doing what you have always done, you will keep get-

ting what you have always gotten." Once you get out of your comfort zone, you can go after your true passions and achieve your dreams.

- **Taking risks will help you will overcome your fear of failure:** This may sound counterintuitive or contradictory, but by taking risks you are facing your fears because they were preventing you from taking the initiative all along. Once you start accomplishing small initiatives and taking small risks that lead you towards your ultimate goal, you will wonder why you had waited so long to take action!

Brendon Burchard, author of *The Charged Life*, describes a process of overcoming our three biggest fears. When we are taking initiatives towards achieving our goals and taking risks that will change our lives, we must overcome our three biggest fears:

1. **Loss Pain:** This pain is the fear of losing what we already have. If we take action or take a risk, we might lose the things that we already have and may never recover them. These things might include:

    - Our relationships with our co-workers
    - Our work environment

- Our friendships
- Our title
- Our 401K
- Corner office
- Respect of our peers
- Our spouses
- Our relationships with our children
- Our possessions

If we change careers or decide to lose weight, leave a relationship or start one, we are afraid of what we may lose. This pain causes us not to act or risk change.

2. **Process pain:** This pain describes how we are afraid to act or risk change since we don't know where to start when we change. We don't know how to start our own business. We don't know who to turn to for support. We don't know how much it will cost to be successful. We are afraid that we might not know how to complete the process. When we decide to break a physical addiction to a substance or alcohol, for example, we know that we will probably experience pain and symptoms of withdrawal when we stop.

3. **Outcome pain**: This pain describes how we fear what will happen if we do take action and take risks

to change our lives, our behavior and our relationships and then end up with the same thing we had before we took action. What if we go through all of this work and the outcome is no better than what we had when we started? We get stuck thinking what if the grass isn't greener on the other side. Then the outcome at the end of all of our work would be no better than what we had originally. We don't take action because we are afraid of what we may or may not get after we take action to change.

What if the Grass Isn't Greener on the Other Side?

Taking risks is the only way to get through these three types of pain. If we take control of our lives and learn that change and challenges can be invigorating, we can change our entire perspective. Instead of dwelling on loss, process and outcome pains, we can learn to visualize and expect all of the gains we will receive through our efforts. If we focus on positive outcomes, we can give our attention to gains that we will receive if we take action. If we start our own business and leave our regular job, we can achieve financial freedom and be able to afford the things we always wanted! If we expect to lose the weight, we can expect to fit into the clothes we always wanted to wear and improve our lifestyle once we succeed. If we break that addiction that has been running our lives, we can experience a healthier lifestyle and learn to reconnect with loved ones and friends whom we may have neglected.

ASK FOR MORE

Action Steps

1. Start taking small risks towards achieving your desired outcome. For example, if you want to start your own business, visualize what it is that would most fulfill you. Will you be creating a product that you want to market or offering a service? If you want to improve your health, what are your goals? Do you want to start restricting your diet or increase your fitness levels through exercise?
2. Take a few emotional risks. Clear up a disagreement that has been lingering between you and another person. Go ahead and risk rejection and try to make amends.
3. Take a risk at work by speaking up in a meeting or discussing an issue that has been bothering you with a co-worker, or a process that you think should change, however minor.

4 Now What? Commit to Your Dream!

Once you decide to ask for responsibility, take the initiative and weigh the risks involved in taking action, it's time to commit to your resolution to change your life. Your level of commitment should reflect your desire and ambition to achieve your goal. At work, we commit to completing reports by imposed deadlines. We are being held accountable to supervisors or superiors. Our level of commitment to completing a task affects us directly, so we may strengthen our commitment to complete the work. Students complete homework assignments and turn them in on time because they are committed to getting a good grade in the class and on their final transcript. Your commitment must be absolute and final. It should bind you emotionally or intellectually to a project or goal. It must be strong and sewn into your heart for you to realize it successfully.

Commitment to anything shows up in your behavior and your actions. If you are committed to a mediocre existence, an average marriage, an average job, and salary, then your level of commitment will be reflected in your behavior. You will do just enough to maintain the average. You will work the required hours expected of you at your job, and complete the work you're assigned. In your marriage or your relationships, you will maintain the relationship for as long as possible so long as it meets your needs. You will spend just enough time with your friends and family, just enough to keep them going.

However, if you commit to a life of excellence and personal satisfaction, this commitment will also appear in your life. You will work harder at your job and take more initiative to increase your overall performance. You will try to improve your relationships by spending more quality time with your spouse or partner. You will spend more time with your children and discover that you can learn more from them than they can from you.

ASK FOR MORE

Everything you do in your life is dependent on your personal commitment. If you can make and keep your commitments, you will earn the trust and respect of others. There is no substitute for a committed life since you only have one. Commit to all aspects of your life to experience positive change.

Whenever you want to exercise your will to commit to any goal, you can start doing the activity in manageable segments. If it is your goal to lose weight, start by eating more fruits and vegetables. Cut or taper off your consumption of fast foods. Join a gym to exercise 2–3 times a week. Some people are always on a diet, but they never lose weight because they didn't commit to making the goal happen. They start to make excuses as to why they failed; they lie to themselves until the next attempt. The problem lies in their level of commitment. Full stop. You will get out what you put into your project, your goal, and it all depends on your level of commitment.

Robert Anthony said:

"Waiting is a trap. There will always be reasons to wait. The truth is, there are only two things in life, reasons, and results, and reasons simply don't count."

If we wait to take action, we might never pursue our lifelong goals, and then it will be too late. No one wants to hear about the reasons why you didn't commit. People look up to those who have made commitments to achieve their goals and shown them the results of their actions. We want to be inspired to change ourselves! We want to see results!

Your actions always speak louder than your words. Your behavior and actions will either embrace your commitment to your goal or your behavior and actions will embarrass you. When you commit yourself to something, you invest yourself fully into your project, idea, product, service, relationship or goal. You give it your best. You know in your heart that there is someone out there who might beat you to it. If you quit before you achieve your goal, you won't reach success. You won't see instant success or a perfect finished product right away. You have to commit to your vision and keep trying to get it right. True commitment allows us to grow to fulfill our most basic dreams and gives us a sense of purpose in our lives.

Throughout modern history, there have been great leaders, explorers, and innovators who committed to making a contribution to the world through their actions:

- Christopher Columbus was committed to finding a Western sea route to Cathay (China) and India and uncovering the riches of India, namely gold and spices. After being rejected by King John II

ASK FOR MORE

of Portugal once and the Spanish monarchy twice, he made his case for the exploration. With three ships and a crew of 39 men, he returned to Spain one year later with gold, spices and other finery. The monarchy exalted him as being the first European explorer of the New World.

- Hernan Cortez followed in the footsteps of Columbus (almost literally) when he set sail in 1519 to the Mexican coast of the Yucatan that had been settled by the Spanish. After a few months, he headed west to conquer the island of Veracruz. His resolve to take the island was so absolute and his commitment so strong that he ordered his soldiers to burn their ships so as to make retreat impossible.

- In 1961, President John F. Kennedy declared that the U.S. would send a man to the moon within the next decade. He convinced Congress to commit $7-9 Billion over the next five years, proclaiming, "This nation should commit itself to achieving this goal, before the decade is out, of landing a man on the moon and returning him safely to earth."

- Henry Ford committed his life's work to making automobiles affordable for every American. Ford said, "I will build a car for the great multitude. It will be large enough for the family, but small enough for the individual to run and care for. It will be constructed of the best materials, by the best men to be hired, after the simplest designs that modern engineering can devise. But it will be so low in price that no man making a good salary will be unable to own one."

What is your level of commitment to your goals? Can you affirm these five statements?

1. I believe that if I work hard and apply my abilities and my talents, I will be successful.
2. I regularly set goals and make sure my needs and those of others around me are met.
3. When working on my goals, I put in maximum effort and work even harder if I suffer a setback.
4. I always create a powerful vision of my success when I work on my goals and hold that vision while I strive to achieve them.
5. I believe that my level of commitment to my goals and objectives will positively affect all of the outcomes and results that I hope to attain.

Action Steps

1. Make a small commitment every day for seven days. For example, take the stairs to the office instead of the elevator. Engage in a conversation for thirty minutes with a friend, spouse or child. Read for 20-30 minutes every day to improve your education.
2. Make one large commitment that you have been putting off for years. Ask yourself why you stopped. What is different now? What small steps could you take to build momentum towards its completion?
3. Read the five commitment affirmations for 30 days and keep your goals and objectives in mind and see what happens.

WHAT'S YOUR MOTIVATION?

In 1923, when asked why he was trying to climb Mount Everest, British mountaineer George Mallory (1886-1924) answered, "Because it's there. Everest is the highest mountain in the world, and no man has reached its summit. Its existence is a challenge. The answer is instinctive, a part, I suppose, of man's desire to conquer the universe" Mallory was modest because by that point in his life he was an experienced climber. In 1910, he and his partner Andrew Irving attempted to climb Mount Velan in the Alps; however, they were forced to turn around because of altitude sickness and other health concerns. In 1911, he climbed Mount Blanc and also made the third ascent of Mount Maudit. In 1913, he climbed Pillar Rock in the English Lake District. In Asia, Mallory led an expedition in 1921 known as the *British Reconnaissance Expedition* financed by the Mount Everest Committee. He and a group of around 12 Sherpas climbed several lower mountains near Everest. During the actual climb of Mount Everest in 1924, Mallory and Irving were last seen around 800 feet from the summit of Mount Everest and disappeared near the North East Ridge of the highest mountain in the world. George Mallory's remains were found 75 years later on May 1, 1999, and people still don't know if he actual made it to the top of Mount Everest. Years before he attempted the climb to the summit of Mount Everest, Mallory was quoted in the Alpine Journal after a successful climb in the Alps as saying: "Have we vanquished an enemy? None but ourselves."

Years later, 650 people climbed Mount Everest after rigorous training exercises and learning how to survive in various degrees of high altitude for months or even years. The question that always remains: "What is their motivation?" Why do people risk their lives to climb a mountain? Over the years, the answers haven't changed that much.

Vanquishing the Enemy Within

Since climbing offers the mountaineer many series of physical, mental and emotional challenges out in the beautiful wild, overcoming these challenges offers the climber an immense sense of personal accomplishment. During the process of preparation, training, and the actual climb, there is an enormous sense of self-awareness and growth. We want to face and overcome our inner fears, push ourselves to the limit and create our best self in the process.

Time to Grow

Because climbing offers the mountaineers so many challenges, the need to learn and develop one's skill set inspires learning, growth and personal development. Serious climbs such as Mount Everest require focused discipline, training, planning and teamwork. These skills apply to other areas of one's life such as business, family, and personal relationships. Although mountain climbing is perceived to be a solitary sport, the group dynamic is crucial to a successful climb.

Because I Can Do It

Mountaineering has come a long way since George Mallory's time. The use of technology, GPS and tracking systems, weather systems, rescue routes, safety equipment, lightweight gear, sophisticated equipment, and experienced guides have made mountain climbing more accessible to more people who have the resources to do it. Still, climbing is all about managing risk. Many climbers want to use all of themselves and their drive and ambition to conquer risk and achieve their dream of getting to the summit.

The study of motivation involves understanding why we do things. When we find our motivation or the reasons why we want to accomplish something in our lives, we take action. Our motivation becomes our driving force and our purpose. Once we can find our why or our reason for continuing, nothing can stop us. Our motivation becomes our reason for living, or as the French say, our "raison d'etre" (reason for being).

In the example of the mountain climbers, there were three reasons behind their motivation to climb mountains:

1. Personal growth and development
2. Learning about themselves and working with others
3. Managing risk and facing a challenge.

The 650 climbers who attempted to climb Mount Everest in 2015 were doing it for the intrinsic rewards which were the outcomes of their behavior, namely the personal satisfaction they got from preparing, training and ultimately, climbing the mountain.

Motivation can either be intrinsic or extrinsic. Intrinsically motivated behaviors come from the sense of personal satisfaction that the person experiences while doing them. Extrinsically motivated behaviors come from the individual receiving a reward for those behaviors. These rewards are given or bestowed upon the individual for the successful outcome of their behavior and actions.

Intrinsic Motivators

- Satisfaction
- Curiosity
- Creativity
- Challenge
- Meaning
- Cooperation and Teamwork
- Competition

Extrinsic Motivators

- Money
- Recognition
- Attention

- Praise
- Medals
- Good grades
- Certificates of Achievement/Participation
- Trophies
- Fame

So, which type is the best motivator, intrinsic or extrinsic rewards? In 1973 social psychologists Mark R. Lepper, David Greene, and Richard Nisbett decided to conduct an experiment with preschoolers to answer the question. The experimenters gave the children felt-tip markers and divided them into three groups: one group was told that they would get a certificate with a gold star in exchange for their drawing. One group wasn't told that they would get a certificate for their drawing but got one when they completed it. The third group was given the markers and the paper and were encouraged to draw pictures, but received no reward. The children who expected a reward for their drawings stopped after a while because their intrinsic rewards for drawing had diminished. The ones who didn't get a reward continued drawing because they enjoyed it. Maybe the kids felt that the reward wasn't worth it. When we do something that we enjoy doing already an external reward diminishes our general interest in the activity.

ASK FOR MORE

Since I was 16 years old, I ran long distance races and completed 41 marathons (26.2 miles). Every finisher received extrinsic rewards such as a T-shirt, a medal, and a certificate. In the case of marathon running, which includes months of preparation and training, the intrinsic rewards far outweigh the extrinsic rewards. Long distance runners commit to the marathon six months in advance and prepare arduously for the big race. They sacrifice countless hours of training, running 40-75 miles per week leading up to the race and often run for stretches of 18-20 miles at a time during the remaining four weeks leading up to race day. Runners run the marathon because of the challenge involved and the physical, emotional and mental challenges involved in being able to conquer the distance. They run the marathon because they want to grow personally, mentally and physically. They complete the race because they can manage the risks and commit themselves to accomplishing their goal.

What is your mountain? What is your marathon? What is your goal? Are you pursuing your dreams? Are there things in life that you want to accomplish? Do you want to reach your full potential? Find your motivation. Ask yourself why you are continuing at your current position and weigh the intrinsic rewards and the extrinsic rewards to see if you would like to improve or change your life. Do what you love to do! Do what makes your heart sing!

ASK FOR MORE

Action Steps

1. Think of a goal you want to accomplish. Make a list of all of the extrinsic rewards and the intrinsic rewards that you would receive if you accomplished your goal. Decide if you are ready to take action now.
2. For seven days commit to practicing random acts of kindness such as helping a friend move, or letting someone in front of you at the checkout line, or buying lunch for a hungry stranger and discover the feeling of intrinsic motivation.
3. Over the next three to four weeks, commit to losing ten pounds. You will discover extrinsic motivators such as recognition and praise from your peers, and intrinsic motivators such as a sense of accomplishment, and better health. Try it; it works!

Ask For Increase

Engagement and Expectations!

In the last chapter, we reviewed intrinsic and extrinsic motivators, and how either consciously—especially when money is a factor—or unconsciously, we do things to obtain those rewards. Intrinsic rewards are those that make us feel good about ourselves on the inside, such as personal growth or satisfaction. Extrinsic rewards are those that come to us from the outside or an external source, such as money or recognition. Engagement is when employees feel psychologically committed to the job and work towards its overall benefit and progress. While money is still an extrinsic motivator which determines people's actions and behavior, many employers overlook employee engagement and intrinsic factors such as personal satisfaction with their jobs.

Many people still believe that the hardest workers make the highest salaries. The truth is those who find joy in what they do make the highest salaries. They strive to improve themselves and their performance to benefit the overall productivity of their organization. When employees are highly engaged, they are highly productive. According to a recent Gallup study, employers who engage their employees set expectations for them. Those expectations, in turn, improve the quality of the employees' expectations of themselves and the performance on the job.

When setting expectations for employees, Gallup offers the following four suggestions:

1. **Work together**. Managers and supervisors should work with their teams to get feedback regarding various group projects. This way, workers will feel that their ideas are heard and will be more vested in expectations and outcomes on the job.
2. **Clarity**. Managers and supervisors must be clear about their expectations of their employees. This way, employees can base their outcomes on these expectations.

3. **Raise the bar.** Employees are not only interested in doing the minimum amount of work. Managers and supervisors should raise standards to motivate their employees to base their expectations on those of their top performers.
4. **Personalize it.** Set expectations which correlate with employees' strengths. Doing so will increase both employee performance and engagement.

General Electric Company

For many years, behaviorists and organizational psychologists have studied behavior on the job to see what external forces, if any, might improve engagement to increase productivity and employee expectations. Between 1920 and 1930, the General Electric Company conducted a famous study at their Hawthorn Plant in Cicero, Illinois. The research scientists wanted to determine if productivity would improve among plant workers if the workrooms were better lit than they were previously. Employees would be more alert; they would see better and, consequently, work better.

Productivity on the job did increase through improved lighting, but what was more interesting was what happened in the control group. In another workroom at the plant where lighting was decreased at certain intervals, productivity increased anyway. Simply by making participants aware that they were part of an experiment stimulated them to work harder. If workers are being appreciated or recognized by their supervisors, they will feel more engaged, and overall productivity will rise. Can we all use the illusion of the Hawthorn effect to raise our expectations? Can we induce ourselves to increase our productivity and increase our expectations?

I remember working as a ceramic tile salesman. There was a beautiful showroom upstairs, and those sales representatives worked with higher profile clients such as architects and contractors. I was hired to work in the bargain basement of the company, selling remnants, end of lots, and high-quality products short on volume. These products were not enough for a building that had ten kitchens, but there may be enough for a few kitchen splash backs behind the sink. Another guy and I were hired at the same time. My boss took me aside and said, "Richard, listen, we're putting you on an hourly rate and a commission for sales because you're a sharp salesman. But hey, don't tell Steven because he is only being paid hourly."

When he told me that I was a sharp salesman, I felt great! I was a new man. I put in extra effort on the job, and I was just selling tiles! I walked the aisles of the warehouse, got to know the inventory and the pricing per square foot of all of the items. I even laid some of the titles on the floor because I wanted to see how they looked together and practiced how to sell the tiles to prospects. A couple of days later while walking through the warehouse, I saw Steven talking with my customer. The day before, my customer had bought some terra cotta tiles, 18" X 18," nice pieces, real beauties for a patio and told me that he would be back for more. I greeted the customer and excused Steven and took him aside. I said, "I think you are working with my customer." He replied, "Your customer? Aren't you being paid hourly?"

Our manager had told him the same thing so that we would come to work on time, stay until closing, and connect with customers to sell them products. He raised our expectations through subtle manipulation. Had he told us the same thing at the same time, we would not have competed for customers' attention, nor would we have worked as hard to meet their needs.

In the workplace and at school, many comparisons have been made to Pygmalion. In a narrative written by Ovid, Pygmalion was a sculptor who carved a woman out of ivory and fell in love with it. So enamored was Pygmalion with his ivory creation that he offered blessings and promises of personal sacrifice at Aphrodite's altar at Aphrodite's festival that he would be able to find a bride similar to the one he loved, the statue. When Pygmalion returned home that night, the sculptor kissed the statue and found her lips were warm. Aphrodite fulfilled the sculptor's wish, and he bore a child with his bride.

This legend has come to represent that higher expectations will lead to an increase in performance and more positive outcomes. Harvard Professor Robert Rosenthal tested this idea. He studied how teacher expectations can affect student performance in a controlled experiment in an elementary school in California. Rosenthal took the *Flanagan Test of General Ability*, a general IQ test, and changed the covers to the *Harvard Test of Inflected Acquisition*. Rosenthal told teachers that the test served as a predictor as to which kids were going to show an increase in their IQ scores. After Rosenthal had administered the test, he told teachers that certain children, chosen at random, demonstrated a propensity for intense intellectual bloom. Over the course of the following two years, Rosenthal found that teachers' expectations of these children affected their performance outcomes. The teachers were giving the students who they expected to succeed academically more time to answer questions, more feedback, approval, and praise.

At work, supervisors' expectations of the employees or groups of employees who are working on a specific project may affect outcomes. The more employees are engaged in learning and training activities the greater the expectations will be from management, considering the employees' acquiring of new skills. Similarly, to increase employees on the job performance, employers will advocate more manager-employee team building activities which foster trust and mutual obligation.

The Zappos Company uses many different types of extrinsic motivators to show appreciation, recognition, and acclaim for a job well done through small but relevant incentives. These include a co-worker bonus program where you can suggest an employee receive extra money because of the assistance she gave to you on a certain task. The Grant a Wish program is one where employees' wishes such as skydiving, riding a motorcycle or even becoming an American Citizen become company collective goals for the individual employee. Zollars are Zappos currency given to fellow employees to show exemplary work on a particular project. These Zollars may be used within the company to buy other swag such as sunglasses or other company products.

Employees can even self-promote in the company by asking to engage in a 90-day Z-apprenticeship program where they learn all of the new skills and capabilities of a job before actually working in the position full-time. If after the 90 days, management sees the individual can carry out all of the requirements of the new position and the employee wants to stay in this new position, then he or she can stay. If the agreement is not mutual, however, the employee may return to the position held earlier within the company.

Try to find meaning in what you do. The intrinsic motivation that you derive from your job will sustain you. Others will see your example and follow suit. Before you know it, your workplace will be transformed into a collaborative environment where everyone wants to make a contribution of lasting significance to the organization.

Action Steps

1. What are your expectations of yourself? Is there a dream you want to accomplish, a goal that you are trying to achieve?
2. What are some ways to increase your expectations of yourself? Is your personality in line with your dreams?
3. Are you engaged in your job? What would be one motivator that would get you to leave your current job to pursue a dream or lifelong goal?
4. Are people successful because they love what they do or because they work harder than others who do the same thing?

7 I THINK I CAN: THE POWER OF WILL

In the last chapter we looked at engagement and determined that when workers feel connected to their work, it will increase their productivity. We also looked at how controlled expectations can improve the behavior of those we are observing. But what if no one is watching? How can we increase our expectations of ourselves? What is our purpose in life? Why are we here? Many people struggle with the answer from a philosophical or spiritual standpoint. For the sake of utility, and making one's contribution to the world, finding your life's purpose will be the true motivator to take action in your life and demonstrate that purpose to the world.

There are three questions you should ask yourself when considering your life's purpose:

1. What's important to you and why?
2. What are you good at doing?
3. How could the world be improved?

These are the big questions that 98% of us don't want to ask. We don't ask more of ourselves although we know, subconsciously, that we have more to give. We follow the path of least resistance and do what is expected of us. Perhaps under possible threats, we do what is demanded of us. Where would we be regarding innovation, political ideology, culture, and progress were it not for individuals who found their life purpose and acted on it to not only improve their status in their community and the world but by making a small contribution to the world through their life purpose?

Individuals Who Found Their Life's Purpose

The Wright Brothers
Samuel Pierpont Langley (1834-1906) was an American astronomer, physicist, inventor and first director of the Alleghany Observatory in Pittsburgh, Pennsylvania in 1867. He dabbled in building aircraft during his time be-

tween 1896 and 1903. Although Langley received $50,000 from the War Department and $20,000 from the Smithsonian, he failed to develop a piloted airplane. Despite Langley's education, his experience in academia and the funds he received in the form of grants, he was unable to achieve his goal. Orville and Wilbur Wright, brothers out of Dayton, Ohio successfully piloted the first glider in 1902.

The Wright brothers did not get any grants from outside sources or agencies. The brothers, driven by a cause, used the proceeds of their small bicycle shop to fund their dream. They had found their life's purpose which was to create the flying machine and change the course of transportation around the world. Samuel Pierpont Langley, however, was an opportunist. He was pursuing a result and the glory, fame, and fortune that came with making a contribution of this magnitude. The Wright brothers were pursuing their "why," their life purpose, their true contribution to the world—that was the key to their success.

Theodore Herzel

Theodore Herzl (1860-1904) was raised in a middle-class family in Budapest, Hungary. He studied journalism, law and had some success as a playwright and worked for a few years as a journalist and reporter for the New Free Press as a correspondent in Paris for the German newspaper. What inspired Herzl's true purpose was in a news report that he was covering for the paper, the Dreyfus affair. The French accused Jewish artillery captain Alfred Dreyfus of passing military secrets to the Germans. Herzl was confounded by this blatant anti-Semitic act and the chants of "Death to the Jews." This act inspired Herzl to redouble his efforts to build popular support to promote Zionism and the creation of a Jewish state and end the growing anti-Semitism that was brewing in Western Europe at the time.

In late 1895, Herzl published *Der Judenstaat* (The State of the Jews), the Jewish Homeland and argued that Jews should leave Western Europe for other countries where they would be safe like Argentina and preferably Palestine, their ancestral homeland. Herzl believed that only through a Jewish state, could they avoid anti-Semitism, express their culture freely and practice their religion. Until his death, Herzl fought hard for his life purpose which was to promote Zionism and create a homeland for the Jews.

Adam Braun

Adam Braun founded Pencils of Promise. He found a need for education in the developing world. Braun developed the concept of Profitable Purpose where non-profits can act as companies to create working schools in developing countries. His charity has created tangible results by showing donors exactly where their money goes. While developing the charity Braun found that $25 is the amount that educates a child, $10,000 builds one classroom and $25,000 builds a school.

Since 2008, these innovations have lead Pencils of Promise to help educate over 30,000 students around the world. That's purpose that lasts, that endures and hopefully, inspires.

Your Life's Purpose

When you think of your life's purpose, it doesn't have to be anything earth-shattering. It could just be grounded in a belief that you have or a contribution that you want to make to the world. When you know your why or the reason you want to do something, everything else will fall into place.

Let's say you have an idea for a product or service, that's the *what* of the process. Many people know how the product or service is implemented and distributed. However, most don't know their *why*. *Why*, in this sense, is not just to make a profit, the *why* must be greater than you, greater than the sum of all of your employees and their collective efforts. Your why must be a vision seen by all of your founders, employees, distributors and end users. Your why reflects your purpose, your belief, your cause and this mission must be felt and pursued by everyone involved in the process.

By combining your skills, opportunities, and passions, you could hone in on your own life's purpose and make a positive impact on the world. You will start feeling the benefits of working for the greater good. You will tend to achieve your goals faster if you have a clear purpose in life. Clarity will help you share your vision with others who see your why. Clarity will also help others believe in you and what you stand for.

You will tend to make better decisions since those decisions will be based on your life's purpose. Through constantly working on your life's purpose, you will feel more motivated and happier. Your life's purpose will even help to contribute to your overall longevity. The legacy you leave behind will have an impact on generations after you have left this earth.

Once you know your life's true purpose, you will feel a sense of urgency to accomplish it and encourage others to be on your side and help you with your goal. If your dream is big enough, it is big enough to share, and collaboration could always lead to improvements in size, design, scope, affordability and scalability. Departments start to exist at any company or start-up because they support the main mission of the company while serving its one function, whether that function is marketing, sales, development, or some other specialty.

Your life's purpose could create a product or service that could change lives and impact the world with your contribution. You will never know if you have greatness in you unless you get up and do something with your life. Your life's purpose should be pulling you towards it every day. Your life's purpose will give you a long series of goals that will serve to give your life its true meaning. Your contribution will then carry meaning and value to millions of people around the world who stand to benefit from your life, your purpose, and your one true vision.

Action Steps

1. Is there a dream or career path that you were interested in as a child? Take one step towards that goal. Did you want to be a firefighter? Go to your local fire station and volunteer. Take one step and then maybe another.
2. Go to your attic or basement. Take out an old musical instrument that you used to play and see if you've "still got it."
3. Visit your alma mater. Continue your education. Take online classes that you're interested in or live classes at your local college, university, or library. Life is dependent on lifelong learning and personal growth.
4. Look at your relationships. Are you growing with that person? Do you share any dreams with that person? Is it time to re-evaluate the relationship? Find purpose in your relationships.
5. Your life's purpose is a combination of your skills, your passions and the opportunities that you find. Try increasing each one a little bit every day, and you will find that your life purpose will grow!

WILL POWER AND SELF-DISCIPLINE

The reality television show *The Biggest Loser* has aired on NBC since 2004. The reality show pits obese contestants against each other to race to see who will lose the most weight. Seven million people choose to watch the show every week. Those who audition to be contestants number up to 200,000 per season. The show makes over $100 Million in ad sales and fringe products like cookbooks, DVDs and clothing.

In a New York Post article entitled "*The Brutal Secrets Behind The Biggest Loser,*" former contestant Kali

Hibbard who lost 121 pounds is now an outspoken advocate against the show. Hibbard was chosen to be a contestant who lived on the ranch during her stay on the show. The Hummingbird Nest Ranch is a 126-acre ranch that doubles as an equestrian estate in Simi Valley, about 75 miles north of Los Angeles.

As a finalist in the competition, Hibbard immediately began her workout routine, 4 hours straight. Trainers forced contestants to train intensely, engaging in activities such as rowing, weight lifting, kettle bells, treadmills, interval training, Stairmaster, and tire pulling. Trainers would shame contestants into training harder to lose the excess weight faster. Furthermore, contestants were only allowed to eat up to 1,000 calories per day and were forced to eat food provided by the show's sponsor such as Jell-O, Rockstar energy drinks, and Kraft Fat Fee Cheese, much of which had little nutritional value.

Former contestants like Hibbard reported suffering from severe malnutrition after the extreme weight loss which they experienced on the show, once they left. One contestant, Ryan Benson who went from 330 pounds to a stunning 208 was so malnourished he was urinating blood. Also, a study showed that contestants who experienced significant weight loss on the show had regained all of the weight they had lost on the show and some had even gained more on top of their original pre-show weight. The show's format: rapid weight loss through intense dieting and exercise, slowed down contestants' metabolic rates so far that their metabolisms took years to return to normal.

Knowing all of this, how could 200,000 obese people look to a show like this and its copycats such as fat farms, fat-freezing techniques, gastric bypass surgeries and fad diets in an effort to lose weight? Because losing weight is tough, time-consuming, and takes willpower. Willpower may be defined as the ability to control one's self and one's urges or emotions. As Kelly McGonigal points out in her 2012 book *The Willpower Instinct*, willpower comes down to a series of three challenges: I will, I won't. I want.

1. **I will power challenge**: What is something that you must do, do more of, or stop putting off because you know that doing it would radically change your life?
2. **I won't challenge**: What habit in your life is controlling you and driving you to distraction? What habit would you like to do less of or give up completely to change your health, happiness or success significantly?
3. **I want power challenge**: What is the most important long-term goal you would like to complete or begin to focus all of your energy on right now?

> Even though this important goal means the world to you, is there an immediate want that tempts you or diverts you away from this lifelong goal?

If 200,000 people auditioned for the show each season for 17 seasons, that means 3,400,000 met all three rules of the Willpower challenge. Let's break it down. They met the "I will" challenge because losing weight has become so hard, that it requires attention to improve one's overall health. They met the "I won't" challenge because weight loss requires refraining from fatty, salty and sugary foods that are high in calories. Lastly, they met the "I want" challenge. These people have a long-term goal which is to return to a normal healthy weight that many have not had since their high school days. It is a major challenge. They saw the show as a way to finally take control of their lives! They auditioned for the show because they hoped that the producers, executives, and trainers would take care of their problem for them.

Aside from weight loss, the average adult must deal with many other life challenges, all of which require willpower and self-discipline. In 2011, the American Psychological Association conducted their annual *Stress in America Survey*. Survey participants reported a lack of willpower as the number one reason why they did not follow through with major life changes that required self-control and self-discipline. The seven major challenges included:

- Eating a healthier diet
- Exercising more
- Losing weight
- Reducing stress
- Getting more sleep
- Reducing or eliminating alcohol consumption
- Quitting smoking

I listed them here to show you that these are struggles that everyone can relate to, challenges that everyone has faced at some point in their lives to overcome. Other challenges that we put off may include: saving for retirement, going back to school, starting a new business, and ending a relationship. Depending on the person, all of these activities require some form of willpower.

So, how can we get more willpower to do all of the things that pass the "I will, I won't, and I want challenge"?

The Stanford Marshmallow Experiment

Since willpower is a measurable skill, social psychologists put it to the test. The study was known as the Stanford Marshmallow Experiment, conducted by Stanford psychologist Walter Mischel in the late 1960's. To test delayed gratification in preschoolers, Mischel and his colleagues gave subjects, age 4-6 year-olds, a marshmallow and told them that they could enjoy the treat immediately or wait 15 minutes to get another similar treat. Out of the 600 children who participated in the experiment, almost a third delayed gratification and got a second treat such as another marshmallow, Oreo or pretzel.

The subjects who delayed gratification and waited for the second treat had better life outcomes as adults. Years after the study they had improved test scores, higher educational attainment, lower Body Mass Index (BMI) and other life measures which include financial success as compared to those who did not delay gratification.

Willpower and the Brain

So people with more willpower are happier, in better relationships, make more money, are better able to manage stress, adversity, and change and even live longer. I mean, who wouldn't want that?

First, to understand willpower, we have to dissect the brain and understand what parts of the brain are responsible for emotion and what parts of the brain are responsible for reasoning and logic. The part of the brain that is responsible for emotions, drives, motivation and urges is known as the limbic system. The prefrontal cortex is the part of the brain associated with rational thought and reasoning. It acts as a filter for the limbic system and decides on the best behavioral response. The prefrontal cortex is willpower central, and like a muscle, willpower must constantly be exercised to get stronger. To exercise your willpower, you must start to do things that you don't feel like doing. If you always yield to the limbic system and let your emotions rule your behavior, you will never fully exercise your prefrontal cortex and practice your willpower.

Let's say you go to McDonald's with some friends. You want to start exercising your willpower, so instead of a Big Mac, you order a Southwest Salad with grilled chicken (the crispy version is fried and has extra calories). They know you usually order the Big Mac combo with fries and a coke. You know that is your standard order, but you fight your limbic system. The process looks like this:

1. You've decided "I want to make healthier eating choices."
2. You move your prefrontal cortex into high gear reasoning, "I won't eat foods that are high in calories and will increase my risk of contracting heart disease and pre-diabetes.
3. Then you teach your prefrontal cortex that new food choices are possible for you: "I want to be

more health conscious and will continue to make healthy food choices whether I am out with friends or shopping for groceries or cooking for myself and others."

Lastly, Dr. McGonigal summarizes five steps that will help you develop your willpower:

1. Self- awareness: Know your triggers and when to use all of your willpower to overcome a challenge. Imagine you have been sober for two years, but your boss invites you out for a drink with some of his friends. Do you try to get along with everyone and break your sobriety?
2. Sleep: Get at least eight hours of sleep. Studies have shown that prisoners of war are more likely to give up secrets or names of enemies or even fabricate information to get some rest after long periods of sleep deprivation. Get enough rest so that your willpower will be strong.
3. Meditate: Meditation, or stopping for just five minutes per day, will strengthen your resolve to maintain your willpower for whatever it is you want to accomplish. Sit in a comfortable position and just breathe in and out for five minutes. Deep breathing is very powerful for thought cleansing and regeneration of willpower.

4. Diet and exercise: Eating healthy foods and keeping up some exercise rituals will keep you focused and strong.
5. Visualize your future self: By visualizing your future self as having already accomplished the goal that you want to achieve, your willpower will strengthen through the process.

Action Steps

1. Think of one major challenge that you have been struggling with for years. Now think of one thing you have to do right away to take steps toward changing that behavior.
2. Find a comfortable chair in your office or at home. Block out all distraction and sit upright in a comfortable chair. Set your phone for 5 minutes, then close your eyes and focus on breathing in and then exhaling. Relax completely and block out any thoughts from your mind. Try the process daily for at least seven days.
3. Write a short letter to your future self. Congratulate your future self on accomplishing your lifelong goal or ending that relationship or breaking that addiction that you struggled with for years. Tell your future self exactly how you did it. Mail the letter to yourself and don't open it for six-twelve months until you accomplish your goal(s).

Procrastination and Other Roadblocks

Biggest Loser contestants from past season may now be able to complain that the trainers were hard on them. Or, the producers publicly shamed them on live television. However, when it came right down to it, the trainers and producers got the job done. Before joining the show, the contestants didn't summon the willpower or the self-control to lose the weight to become healthy.

A common obstacle to willpower and self-control is procrastination. Up to 20% of adults have regular periods of procrastination. Procrastination or putting things off is a very common human tendency. Procrastinators are not only putting things off because they may seem unpleasant or hard to do, but they also delay opportunities that could bring them joy, money, love and success.

Chronic procrastinations tend to lose or waste time through their inclination to avoid more productive behaviors. They tend to miss out on various opportunities, thinking that they will return to them at a later date. They tend not to set too many life goals. If they do, they are often hesitant to take the next steps towards achieving those goals. Procrastination tends to ruin or at least hamper a person's career. They tend to miss important deadlines or targets. They make poor decisions by waiting until the very last minute to act, and they earn the reputation of being a late bloomer or one who makes empty promises and always comes up short. Procrastination could ultimately affect one's health since putting things off leads to feelings of regret, stress, guilt, anxiety and depression.

So, if procrastination is so adverse to our mental and physical health and future success, why do we do it? How can we stop procrastinating to achieve our everyday goals and accomplish our lifelong dreams? People procrastinate for different reasons. Dr. Joseph Ferrari, in his aptly-named book, *Still Procrastinating* describes three basic types of procrastinators:

Arousal types: These people like to wait until the last minute to get things done or turn in work by the deadline. They experience a certain thrill or rush by getting things done under the wire.

Avoider types: These people put things off because they are avoiding their fear of failure or even success by completing a special goal or project. They tend to be self-conscious and are overly concerned about what people will think of them. They would rather other people think that they lack the effort than the ability to accomplish tasks which are assigned to them.

Decisional types: These are people who cannot make a decision. By not making an actual decision, these types of procrastinators are released from taking responsibility for the outcome of their actions.

More than 20% of taxpayers wait until the very last minute to submit their income tax return to the IRS. Are they the arousal types, who get a rush by turning things in just before the deadline? Or, are these taxpayers avoiding the task of filing their returns because they owe taxes and are avoiding payment? Perhaps they will prepare their returns early, and they just can't decide between paper or e-filing until the very last minute before the deadline.

We are all usually a combination of all three types depending on the nature of the task that needs to get done, our resources to accomplish the task and our personal motivation to get it done. For example, men and women are increasingly delaying a common adult milestone . . . their first marriage! In the United States, the average age of women who marry for the first time is 27; the average for men is 29. These numbers are up from 23 for women and 26 for men in 1990, and 20 for women and 22 for men in 1960. Future generations will also have to wait a little longer now that women are waiting longer to have their first child. The average age women give birth for the first time is now 26.3 years up from 24.9 years around fifteen years ago.

The Seven Triggers of Procrastination

Here it would be helpful to learn the seven triggers of procrastination to better account for our behavior:

1. You feel overwhelmed by the task. You put it off because you feel you won't have enough time to complete it, or maybe it's beyond the scope of your abilities.

2. You are afraid of success. If you complete the task successfully, will you get an even harder task? Will there be a promotion in your future? Will you have to leave your friends behind?
3. You resent responsibility. Do you feel you're doing someone else's job? Are you doing something that is above your pay grade?
4. You are afraid of failure. Maybe you feel that others will judge you by the completion of the task and if you fail there will be repercussions.
5. You don't know what you're doing. You don't start or take the initiative because you don't know where to begin.
6. You are afraid of an upcoming conflict. You put off the task because it involves another co-worker, a vendor your work with a lot.
7. The task bores you, and you feel it has no real purpose. You put it off because it's too easy for you or it's insulting to you since it's beneath your skill level.

The key to circumventing procrastination is getting started and taking action towards achieving the completion of your goals. Remember to get out of your own way when it comes to deciding to take action towards completing a task at work or achieving a lifelong dream. In the next chapter, I will discuss goal setting, decisiveness and taking action.

Action Steps

1. Describe an incident where you were acting as one of Dr. Ferrari's three procrastinator types: Arousal; Avoider or Decisional. What happened and how do you relate to that type of procrastinator?
2. Many experts say that people procrastinate because of their fear of success. If success is something we all want, how can we be afraid of it? Explain how fear of success has kept you from pursuing a goal or achievement.
3. Think of three things or tasks which you have been putting off. Write them down and beneath each of the tasks, write down three things you will do to complete each one of them.

10 EXECUTION, EFFORT, AND EXCELLENCE

Since I was 16, I have run 41 full marathons. I started running when I was 12. It was 1979, and the running craze was just getting started. Cities around the world were creating international marathons through their streets to attract elite runners from around the world to their cities, promote tourism, and generate income for local sponsors. Given the popularity of the longer distance of 26.2 miles, race organizers starting creating smaller, shorter distance races to accommodate runners who wanted to compete and practice, but weren't ready for the marathon distance. I ran those races, too. I acquired personal bests in the 5K, 10K, 15K, 20K, 30K and Half-Marathon distances. By age 19, I ran a 3:06 marathon. I was in the best shape of my life.

Every race I ever ran began with the application. By filling out the application and sending in the entry fee, I was committing to running the race. After committing to the race, I knew I had to take action towards achieving my goal. Athletes can easily predict what their average mile time has to be to break the tape by a certain time since all running races are timed. For example, I accomplished my best time in the marathon, 3:06, by running 26.2 7-minute miles. The elite runners who consistently run 2:10 marathons are running 5-minute miles the whole way!

Any dedicated marathoner can tell you that training for a marathon is an effort that requires dedication, focus, and sacrifice. If you want to perform at the top of your game, you will have to eat the right foods, get plenty of rest, and drink a lot of water. Furthermore, you must abstain from alcohol when possible and run 50-75 miles a week at least 12 weeks before the marathon date with at least two or three 20-mile runs about a month before the event. It is a grueling experience that requires time, focus and dedication.

We admire celebrities, actors, and professional athletes from afar because they made those sacrifices to find their

ASK FOR MORE

greatness. We wonder how they could have achieved so much in their lives. We think that they must have been born with some innate talent that we will never have. In actuality, they are no different than the rest of us. They became who and what they are because of their decision to look for their greatness and expend the effort necessary that will lead to their success. They decided to expend the effort to make their success possible. The main reason why people are successful is that successful people, be they athletes, singers, actors or entrepreneurs decided to look for their greatness. They expended the extra effort and made sacrifices to reach their goals. They took action towards their highest achievements.

In a segment on *The Tonight Show*, an iconic late-night variety show hosted by Jimmy Fallon called "Would You Rather?" Jimmy played the game against actor Kevin Hart. In the game, Jimmy and Kevin had to decide on what the audience of around 200 would have selected based on their opinion of popular culture. In the question, "Would you rather sing like Beyoncé or run like Usain Bolt?" 67% of the audience would rather sing like Beyoncé than run like Usain Bolt.

The audience's answer, of course, undermines the effort which both people put into their work and careers. Beyoncé started her career in singing and dancing at the age of 7 when she was still living in Texas. She participated in numerous rehearsals and talent shows before a scout spotted her on *Star Search*. Before the singer cut an album with Columbia Records, she had been working in the industry for six years and started her rise to stardom at the tender age of 14.

Like Beyoncé, Usain Bolt, the fastest human in the world worked hard and long to achieve his position in the world. Bolt is an eight-time Olympic gold medalist and winner of the 100 M; 200 M; and 4 X 100 M in three consecutive Olympic games. Bolt began sprinting as a child in his native Jamaica, and by the age of 12, he ran the fastest 100 Meter race at his primary school.

There is, of course, no way to know why two-thirds of a studio audience wanted to sing like Beyoncé. Maybe they thought that if they could sing like her, they could be as successful, famous and wealthy as her. As for those who chose the Olympian sprinter, Bolt, maybe they were impressed with his athletic abilities during the Olympics which aired around the same time as the taping of the show. Or, perhaps they chose him because they wanted to improve their athletic ability or once aspired to be in the Olympics themselves.

We admire people who pursue their dreams, goals, and aspirations. So, why don't we start as well? We all have goals; we all want to make a lasting contribution to our families, our careers, to society or even to the world. We

ASK FOR MORE

are all people living our lives in the pursuit of happiness and fulfillment. Why do so few of us take action to make our mark on the world?

In 1970, Bernard D. Sadow was a vice president at a Boston-based luggage and coats manufacturer. One time upon returning home from a vacation in Aruba with his family, he noticed something in the airport that changed his perspective. He noticed an airport employee pulling a heavy machine on a skid that had wheels underneath it. The wheels made pulling the machine effortless, regardless of its weight. It was then and there that Sadow got the idea to put wheels on the underside of suitcases to make them easier for passengers to transport as they flew and made their connections and transfers. Sadow's idea revolutionized the way passengers carry, use and transport their belongings as they travel around the world.

Another little-known innovator who made an impact on the way we travel was Bob Kearns, a Detroit-based engineer who invented the intermittent windshield wiper. Mr. Kearns saw a need for a wiper that would speed up at different times when the rain was heavier, a simple idea that drivers take for granted today. But, at the time it didn't exist yet. Mr. Kearns worked to build a prototype and develop a patent to align himself with an automobile manufacturer that could mass produce his design and install them on cars. Although many years of his life was tied up in litigation with car manufacturers who adopted his design and changed it, his invention made cars safer in America and around the world.

Similarly, we know little about Joy Mangano. At the age of 34, Mangano, a Long Island, New York divorced mother of three invented the self-wringing mop in 1990. She appeared on the QVC shopping network in 1992 and sold 18,000 units in less than half an hour. Within ten years the mops were generating over $10 Million annually in sales. Mangano went on to develop Forever Fragrant air freshener products, Huggable Hangers and Performance platform shoes. She is the founder of Ingenious Designs and all of her inventions collectively bring in over $150 Million in sales on the HSN (Home Shopping Network).

Are you ready to use your talent? Are you prepared to give the world your gift, your contribution that will make the world a better place? No one else can make your unique contribution but you since it is unique to your life vision. Are you prepared to start here and now and take action towards living your dream and realizing your full potential? It is time to act and make a decision to take control of your life and achieve your goals and ambitions.

Once you decide to take action towards achieving your goal, it will be hard to turn back. When you take action, you grow and learn what works and what doesn't. You start to hone your focus on what fulfills you and what gives you the most pleasure, and the most growth during the experience. The goal and its achievement is not the thing that brings us happiness, but the experience of growth and change that we go through as we are trying to reach the goal that we want. When you are striving towards some accomplishment or goal, you must believe in your purpose and understand why you are doing it. If you feel that your talent or gift is worth cultivating, success is close at hand. If you feel a sense of meaning for what you do, you will work harder than anybody else in the world towards achieving it.

We all have great ambitions, promises that we make to ourselves, but often fail to fulfill. In the case of resolutions, only 8 percent of us reach our goals, according to a 2012 University of Scranton study. Gary Keller, author of *The One Thing* reveals the 1:3:5 rule. Keller says since it is often difficult to achieve our goals because we have so many other commitments and obligations happening at the same time, the 1:3:5 rule helps us to set priorities. Here it is:

- Commit to accomplishing one big thing.
- Identify three priorities that will help you achieve your one big thing.
- Determine five strategies that will help you to accomplish your three priorities.

This process will allow you to break the big goal into smaller manageable steps. The process will also allow you to avoid multi-tasking or working on too many things at the same time, thus separating your attention to different tasks without fully focusing on the one that needs your full attention. Once you implement this process, it will allow you to possibly delegate smaller goals to other talented people while you work on "big picture thinking."

Find your ambition. Find your gift, open it and share it with the world. The time is now. The place is here. If you feel that you have something you want to give to the world and your fellow man, then cultivate your goal, nurture your ambition and start to take action to achieve it. We all start off in this world naked, dumb and speechless. Our drive, our effort, our refusal to fail or give up is what separates us and makes us special.

Action Steps

1. What is your one thing? Building a house; Developing a phone App; Starting a restaurant; Writing a book? Using the 1:3:5 rule, break your main goal down into smaller manageable goals.
2. If a Genie granted you three wishes, what would they be? What's stopping you from achieving those wishes right now?
3. Think of one celebrity that you admire, living or dead, and list the qualities about that person that you most admire. Do you have the same qualities?
4. How can you make yourself better right now? Make a list of ten qualities that you have and ten faults that you would like to improve.

Ask For Character

Courage

Whenever you start out pursuing something new or starting on an important goal, you will find that there will always be people in your life who will try to give you their feedback regarding your plan—sometimes unsolicited! They will want to give you their opinion of your dream and tell you that it's the right thing to do, or tell you if the timing is right, or to judge you to see if you are truly capable of accomplishing it.

Getting others' constructive feedback can be helpful when we are pursuing our goals and aspirations. We must be aware that the feedback they provide is through their filters or perspective and such advice could cloud our judgment as to how we see things and how we want to create our vision for ourselves. When you stand up for yourself and your dreams, it takes tremendous strength and courage to go against what people might expect of you or want from you.

People close to you such as a partner, husband or wife might try to dissuade you because they might feel that you are wasting resources of time and money better spent on other things. If they care about you, they might feel that your endeavor might be burning you out or hurting you physically or emotionally.

Naysayers who discourage you from following your dreams, starting a project or completing a goal might be doing so for some different personal reasons. People you work with might feel threatened if you voice your ideas to break away from the job to pursue your goals. They might also feel alienated by your actions since your current position might not be "good enough" for you but they have to stay. Another thought they might have is wondering what may be wrong with the company itself if someone wants to leave or branch out on their own. They will impose their self-limiting beliefs upon you because they might not have the same passion, mental strength or ambition as you.

ASK FOR MORE

If you should disclose to someone at work that you are considering quitting the job, the "secret" will quickly become a rumor. People from various departments might come up to you to warn you about the economy, your pension or benefits and the tenure and stability that you had built up over the years at the company. Some may prescribe caution since you might not find another position like the one you currently have at a different company. Others might caution you that the nature of doing business has changed since you were hired and you may not be re-hired unless you get new and updated skills. Some, envious of your career move, might say that you are too young and inexperienced or too old and set in your ways to make any major changes to your career.

Every time someone tries to give you any advice after you tell them about your plans consider the source. Be selective about whom you share your goals with, lest your goals are crushed, and you won't start anything. If it's someone you trust and confide in, the advice might be well-warranted and valid. If, for example, you want to start your own business and someone you consider to be a friend tells you, "In this economy? You've got to be crazy! I would never try anything like that!," perhaps that comment stems from fear because maybe your friend just doesn't have the guts to start his own business and is afraid that you will succeed at yours.

When someone tries to offer you friendly "advice" about your dreams, consider if the advice makes actual sense regarding what you are trying to achieve. Also, consider if they have any experience with what you are trying to achieve or know someone who could help you. Maybe this person might want to help you with your goals and even become a possible partner. So consider if the advice or comments will put you in a better position and if the advice is coming from a position of fear or a comforting place of love and admiration.

If you sense that someone is a naysayer, brushing you off right after you have told them about your biggest dreams, then tune them out. Don't engage in any conversation with someone who is going to continue to discourage you from pursuing your plans. Trying to assert yourself to someone who deliberately wants to disagree with you will not resolve anything. The best course of action, in this case, is to switch topics and don't bring it up again with this person because the same conversation will repeat itself.

Try to stay away from people you know will discourage you from pursuing your dreams. At work, find positive people you could spend time with and discuss your plans in a constructive way if the subject comes up in conversation. In your social life, be with like- minded people who might also be pursuing a similar goal so that you could support one another. At home, even your family or spouse may not support you so try to spend time pursuing your dream even if it means spending time away from them. When you are together, don't bring up the subject with them or else they might start an argument and offer up more reasons as to why you should quit.

People Who Have Succeeded Despite the Naysayers

In many cases, the people who love you the most tend to be the most discouraging. The movie, *Invincible* (Disney 2006), chronicles the life of Vince Papale. It is based on the true life events of how the Philadelphia high school teacher and part-time bartender went on to play football for the Philadelphia Eagles team after an open tryout. In the movie, after learning that Papale was laid off from his teaching job, his first wife Janet left him a note in their South Philly apartment saying, "You'll never go anywhere, never make a name for yourself and never make any money." This event led to some dramatic action which showed Mark Wahlberg, the actor who played Vince Papale, redoubling his efforts to get on the team.

There are many other athletes, celebrities, singers and actors who had the courage to confront people who discouraged them from pursuing their dream:

RICHARD BELLMAN

His parents and teachers encouraged Matt Groening, creator of The Simpsons, to find a *real* profession by going to college and doing something else with his life.

Charlie Chaplin grew up in a dysfunctional family. His parents separated when he was three. Hollywood executives later rejected his act because they thought it was too ridiculous for the American viewing audience.

Michael Jordan was cut from his high school basketball team in his sophomore year because he was too short to play on the team.

His school teacher told Thomas Edison that he was "too stupid to learn anything." Subsequently, Edison's mother decided to home-schooled him.

Jimmy Denny, the manager of the Grand Ole Opry, fired Elvis Presley. He told the King: "You ain't going nowhere, son. You ought to go back to driving a truck."
The Beatles were turned down by Decca Records executive Dick Rowe who told them "guitar groups are on the way out."

The Kansas City Star newspaper fired Walt Disney because he "lacked imagination and had no good ideas."

Oprah Winfrey at the age of 22 was told that she was "unfit for TV." Today, her net worth is close to $3 Billion.

You alone are accountable to yourself and should not believe others opinions of you. Never withstand insults or put downs from other people who don't believe in you. We shouldn't need external validation to tell us that we are enough. You are enough for yourself. No matter what your current title or condition, you can overcome any obstacle or condition or circumstance if you believe in yourself. Love yourself enough to escape the prison of your mind and your self-limiting beliefs. Love yourself enough to free yourself from other people's derision and criticism.

If your dream is important enough to you, you don't need anyone to convince you of it. You don't need to prove anyone wrong, or tell the people who tried to crush your dreams, "I told you so!" If your goals are important enough to achieve, then accomplish them for yourself and be accountable only to yourself. When you succeed, all of the people who put you down and tried to tell you that there was no way you could have made it will be changing their story, saying that they knew you could do it all along.

Spend your time with people who are supportive of you and want you to succeed. Even if you can't find anyone who will support your cause, get out and talk about it with strangers at networking events, parties, business mixers, and on social media. There are many ways of garnering support for your vision or your dream. Spreading the word about your plans to other people who express a genuine interest in your cause will help to bolster your ideas in a positive way. The more you talk about your goals and the more realistic they appear to you, the stronger the vision will become until ultimately, it turns into a reality that will benefit thousands, maybe even tens of thousands or millions of people around the world.

Moreover, try to be a mentor or enabler to someone who is looking for professional advice to start a project that you might have experience with. You and your time are the greatest gifts you could give to people around you. The Latin expression, *ensare aprende*, means "He who teaches learns in the process" still holds true. As you teach someone else, you could develop new skills and look at things from a different perspective and then go on to use those new skills yourself. Give of yourself with an attitude of gratitude, and you will reap the benefits throughout your career and your life.

ASK FOR MORE

Action Steps

1. Think of your goal. Write a list of the people you have to tell about it to achieve it.
2. Now, think of your goal and write a list of ten reasons why you want to achieve it.
3. Write your obituary. Make a list of all your achievements as if they have already been accomplished and describe the legacy that you plan to leave behind.

Faith

In the 2011 movie, *Limitless*, Bradley Cooper plays an aspiring author, Eddie Mora who is down on his luck. Mora suffers from writer's block and can't seem to write anything that has any lasting value—that is until he runs into his ex-brother-in-law who gives him a pill called NZT. The pill allows Eddie to tap into his full human potential and become truly limitless, so long as he has access to the drug. He can remember absolutely everything he has ever read. He can learn a new language in 24 hours. He decides to become a highly successful day trader because of his newfound skills for parsing complex economic equations and deciphering how stocks will react in the short-term based on their long-term performance and the climate of the market. He can accomplish all of these feats as long as he has access to NZT.

I believe the author's main message is that we all have our limitless potential to reach our greatness. But like the main character in the movie, we feel blocked, stilted, paralyzed, even. We stand in our way of reaching our greatness. Maybe we feel we aren't worthy of greatness. Maybe we don't believe in ourselves enough to reach our full potential to be successful and fulfilled. We need faith to reach our potential. We need to believe in ourselves fully and completely to reach our goals and accomplish our true potential in life.

We are all limitless. We have unlimited potential, in spite of ourselves. We must stop, or at least control our negative self-talk that is part of the 50-70,000 thoughts that stream through our minds every day. We must believe in ourselves more completely and eliminate the self-limiting beliefs that we tell ourselves. We talk ourselves out of our dreams and highest aspirations. We limit the scope of our biggest dreams. Instead of thinking as big as we can, we limit our vision to what we think we're capable of and fall short of our dreams.

The only way to overcome the fears, inhibitions, and doubts that you might have when you are undertaking new challenges is to dig in and believe in yourself and your abilities. At times, we get stuck. We find refuge in our self-limiting beliefs and find a way out of our dreams. We create reasons why we can't achieve our highest dreams and aspirations. Before we begin, we talk ourselves out of it.

The Top Ten Self-Limiting Beliefs

- I'm too old.
- I'm not smart enough.
- I'm not educated enough.
- I'm afraid I might fail.
- You need money to make money, and I'm broke now.
- I've already tried everything, and nothing ever seems to work in my favor.
- It's selfish to even want more. I'm content with what I have.
- I don't feel that I deserve it.
- I don't have the willpower necessary to follow through on my goals.
- When it comes right down to it, all the good jobs, opportunities, careers and franchises are taken.

If these self-limiting beliefs sound familiar, it's because you have used some of them to avoid completing a goal that you wanted to achieve for yourself probably. In fact, you may be able to add even more self-limiting beliefs to the list. People blame the economy, their spouse, their business partner, friends or neighbors. Personal accountability always trumps blaming and complaining about your current situation. Find your strengths and believe in yourself and you can achieve anything you want out of life. You are limitless so long as you can believe in yourself.

Self-Efficacy

Believing in yourself is not just a form of self-motivation. Positive psychology experts have studied the field of Self-Efficacy as developed by Stanford psychologist Albert Bandura in his ground-breaking 1977 white paper, *Self-Efficacy: Toward a Unifying Theory of Behavioral Change*. Bandura definition:

> *"Self-efficacy is the belief in one's capabilities to organize and execute the courses of action required to manage prospective situations."*

If you believe you can achieve something then this belief will determine how you think, behave and feel. Naturally, people with a strong sense of self-efficacy take on challenging tasks; are deeply involved in activities they take on; have a strong sense of commitment to these activities and recover quickly from failures or roadblocks which they encounter.

ASK FOR MORE

Bandura explained that there are four ways people judge their self-efficacy: Performance Outcomes; Vicarious Experiences; Verbal Persuasion and Physiological Feedback.

Performance Outcomes: Bandura states that past experiences or performance outcomes are the best source of self-efficacy. If you were successful doing a particular task, then you will try it again because you know you can do it.

Vicarious Outcomes: People can develop high self-efficacy by watching someone in a similar position perform a certain task or complete a goal and then measure competence and skill against someone else's work. A good example of this factor is mentorships in which individuals receive guidance and advice as they complete a task

Verbal Persuasion: Self-efficacy is always affected by positive encouragement and praise. If a manager or any supervisor praises an employee on work that they did, they will continue to work in the same fashion. On the other hand, if a manager scolds an employee for work that not completed properly, the employee will not engage in this kind of work or task, because they obviously failed.

Physiological Feedback: When performing a certain task, people receive physiological feedback from their bodies as they perform. The sensations they experience while performing indicates how they will perform at doing the task. For example, if you are giving a speech in front of a large audience, you might feel anxious and have an accelerated heartbeat.

While understanding the psychology of self-efficacy can help us to figure out why believing in yourself is important to the success of your accomplishments, sometimes, believing in your goal and knowing that you are the only one who can accomplish it will ultimately lead you to success.

People who believe in themselves and their goals overcome setbacks, failures, and obstacles to achieve their dreams. They overcome their failures because they see them as stepping stones to accomplishing their biggest dreams. People who have achieved wild success persevered despite personal and financial failures.

- Albert Einstein didn't speak a word until he was four years old.
- Actor and comedian, Jim Carrey, dropped out of school to support his family when he was 15 years old. Carrey lived with his family in a van at the time.
- Benjamin Franklin dropped out of school when he was only ten. He was an autodidactic student and a voracious reader, so he was undeterred by this obstacle.

ASK FOR MORE

- Richard Branson is dyslexic. He was a poor student. He focused on his charisma and his belief in himself and ideas enough to create Virgin airlines and other companies. He is now the fourth richest person in the world.
- Stephen King's first novel *Carrie* was rejected in the mid-1970's by 30 different publishing houses. Ready to give up, he threw the manuscript in the trash, but his wife retrieved it and urged him to complete it. King's books have sold over 350 million copies.
- Jay-Z always believed in himself. He knew that one day he would become a famous rapper. He approached many different record labels and was turned down over and over again. He decided to create his label called Roc-A-Fella records and would sell records outside record stores to build a following. Now his net worth is at $500 Million.
- Although Vincent Van Gogh only sold one painting while he was alive, he painted over 900 works of art. His persistence is emblematic of his belief in himself. He was a true artist who was committed to his craft.

Your opinion of yourself becomes your eventual reality. If you doubt yourself, then no one will believe in you, and everything will go wrong. If you think the opposite, then you will be able to accomplish anything that you set your mind to, and you will be able to overcome any obstacles that are in your way. Remember, the higher your self-belief, the higher your power to transform your dream into reality. By having supreme confidence in yourself and your abilities, you will be able to achieve anything.

To achieve success in any endeavor, you must believe that you can succeed no matter how the odds are stacked against you. You must look past all of your self-limiting beliefs and start finding your strengths to realize your goals. If you believe that you can achieve it, then you will. You owe it to yourself; you owe it to the world.

ASK FOR MORE

Action Steps

1. Is there a self-limiting belief that is standing in your way? What if things were different?
2. Are you limitless? Make a list of all the things you can do.
3. Do you have a strong sense of self-efficacy? How has this helped you throughout your career?

13 PATIENCE

John Augustus Roebling was the original creator of the Brooklyn Bridge. Roebling was born in Germany in 1806. He studied civil engineering in Berlin and moved to Western Pennsylvania at the age of 25. Based in Harrisburg, he worked as a civil engineer. He also established a wire-cable factory.

He established himself in the Pennsylvania region as a designer of suspension bridges. He designed the Allegheny Aqueduct Bridge in Pittsburgh in 1844; the Smithfield Street Bridge in Pittsburgh in 1886; the Allegheny Bridge in Pittsburgh in 1859; and the John A. Roebling Suspension Bridge, connecting Cincinnati, Ohio to Covington,

RICHARD BELLMAN

Kentucky over the Ohio River in 1886. He is most known for his design of the Brooklyn Bridge in 1883.

The Brooklyn Bridge in New York City is one of the oldest suspension bridges in the United States. The bridge connects Manhattan and Brooklyn by spanning the East River. At its opening in 1903, the Brooklyn Bridge was considered the longest suspension bridge, measuring 1,595 feet (486.3 M) and the first steel-wire suspension bridge. The Brooklyn Bridge is now over 125 years old. It has become an iconic part of the New York skyline, and over 150,000 vehicles and pedestrians cross over it every day.

The bridge's construction was approved in 1867 and just before construction was about to start John A. Roebling was injured on the job site. A boat crushed his foot, and he died of tetanus three weeks later. Washington Roebling, age 32, took over the project as the chief engineer. He had worked alongside his father on many projects and had even helped design the Brooklyn Bridge.

Workers, known as "sandhogs" were mainly immigrants who earned $2 per day for their arduous work on the bridge. Workers excavated the riverbed in massive wooden boxes known as caissons. These airtight structures made it difficult for them to breathe and they often developed respiratory illnesses since they breathed in the air while working in the caissons and also absorbed dangerous amounts of gas into their bloodstreams throughout the

ASK FOR MORE

construction of the bridge. Because of this many workers developed joint pain, paralysis, convulsions, and numbness of the body and speech impediments. Among the 100 workers to develop "caissons disease" Washington Roebling remained paralyzed for the rest of his life. He oversaw the construction of the bridge with a telescope as his wife Emily took charge of the construction process. By the time the bridge opened in 1903, construction had taken 14 years; 600 workers were involved; 25 people died from caissons disease and other accidents, and the cost was $15 M ($320 Million in today's dollars).

I presented this example to show how important patience is when completing any endeavor of lasting value. Obviously, building a bridge, especially one the size and magnitude of the Brooklyn Bridge took time and tremendous effort to complete. Anything of lasting value takes time and patience to complete. Washington Roebling felt compelled to complete the construction of the bridge despite being paralyzed and forced to the confines of his home. The fact that he chose to live within view of the bridge and oversee the operation with the aid of a telescope and only trusted the actual hands-on supervision of the bridge's construction to his wife speaks volumes about his dedication to the project and respect for his father's legacy. Many people who feel personally attached to a project don't give up its completion or delegate the project to someone they trust, someone qualified enough to complete what had been started. There was no one else who could be trusted to complete the project, no trusted foreman or supervisor who could complete the project. No one could be chosen to complete a Roebling bridge but a Roebling. He had the patience and the foresight to keep the bridge in the family. Because of his illness, and the symptoms and side effects that followed, the Brooklyn Bridge was the last Washington Roebling project.

Success never happens overnight. Regardless of talent, effort, connections, education or experience, success doesn't just come to a person. It must be earned over time through consistent effort. Patience is a virtue in any field because through having patience one can overcome obstacles, failures, and pitfalls while striving towards one's goals and objectives. It is frustrating when we try to reach our goals, and they seem so out of reach. We wonder why it is so hard to get what they want. Without patience, it is all too easy to give up on our dreams, our aspirations and ultimately to give up on ourselves.

By practicing patience, we can celebrate small triumphs as we wait for our larger goal to realize. Through patience, we can practice trial and error and learn from our mistakes. By being patient for our larger goal, we can perfect our stepping stones, aspects about ourselves that we want to change, and learn to forgive our shortcomings and accept other people. If gratification were instant, there would be no journey, no growth through our experiences. By having patience, you are building your psychological reliance for success. Knowing that success is a slow process, your patience will allow you to perfect your skills, your finished product and accomplishments. Patience will allow you to grow stronger through the realization of some of your goals as you strive towards the pinnacle of your biggest aspirations.

Depending on your definition of success, it could take years or decades to accomplish. You must be willing to put in the effort to accomplish your goals no matter how long it takes. You have to be willing to keep on putting in the hours to achieve mastery and reach your goals. Never stop learning, never stop questioning, and never stop growing as you work towards your biggest dreams.

Success isn't always a linear process. Our goals mature as we age. Our priorities change as we grow and develop and as we increase our skills. Many people achieved success later in life. If you practice patience, success can taste just as sweet.

Harlan "Colonel" Sanders held down various jobs for 40 years before opening up his first service station in 1930. He fried chicken for weary travelers who stopped for gas at his service station, but it wasn't until 1952 when Sanders sold his first Kentucky Fried Chicken franchise. He was 62 years old. At the time of his death in 1980, there were over 6,000 KFC franchises in 40 countries.

In 1955, the McDonald's brothers enjoyed a simple life. They owned two hamburger restaurants that served hamburgers, cheeseburgers, and French fries. Customers washed down these delicacies with milkshakes. That's where Ray Kroc came in. Ray Kroc sold milkshake machines to restaurants and diners. He went out to San Bernardino from his native Chicago because he wanted to know why they needed eight milkshake machines. Impressed with the brothers' clean restaurant, limited menu, and self-service model, Kroc bought the brothers out in 1961. At that time, he was 59 years old. By the time of his death in 1984, McDonald's had become the most recognizable fast food restaurant in the world. There were 7,500 locations in 31 countries, and he was worth $8 Billion.

Dr. Peter Mark Roget was born in London in 1779 and practiced medicine until 1840. After his retirement, he spent the next 15 years compiling words that had similar meanings and compiled and published the *Thesaurus of English Words and Phrases* in 1852 when he was 73. Over the next 15 years until his death at 90, he continued to work on the next 25 editions of *Roget's Thesaurus*, a must resource for libraries, bookstores and college dorm rooms around the world.

ASK FOR MORE

So, take your time and allow your best, true self to unfold as you pursue your dreams and reach your goals. Patience is a virtue that is required for you to overcome obstacles, failures, and setbacks. Patience will get you through periods of uncertainty and doubt. Once you are successful, you will wonder why you were ever in a hurry.

Action Steps

1. How can having patience help you learn more about yourself?
2. Is being too old a self-limiting belief? Can success be achieved at any age?
3. Practice your patience every day by visualizing how you want things to turn out. If you are in traffic, or in a long meeting, or in line at the bank or grocery store, take your mind off the situation at hand and visualize the outcome you most desire. Pretty soon, patience will be a habit.

14 INTEGRITY

When we think of someone who has integrity, we think of someone who is honest and straightforward. Integrity means adherence to a set of values and principles that are in line with one's goals and aspirations, while self-integrity means being true to your values, beliefs, and convictions. Most of the time, we don't even have to voice our true values or beliefs to others because they are reflected through our behavior and our actions.

Our values are defined by our choices and actions. For example, if we say that we want to lose weight, but find that we are accepting invitations to eat out every day, then our beliefs don't align with our actions, and our self-integrity is at stake. Also, if others observe us behaving contrary to what we say are our beliefs, they most likely won't follow us and are likely to think less of us in the process.

If we live our lives with integrity to ourselves, and what we believe in, then we can build and create trust with others. Once we can do the things we say we are going to do, our lives will have a greater meaning. People will follow us for what we stand for and the actions that reflect our core values.

Self-integrity is a practice that must be honed and developed. In pursuing one's dreams and aspirations, it is crucial to maintain a high level of self-integrity. We often lie to ourselves because we want to make allowances for our inaction and excuse ourselves for our lack of success.

Cognitive Dissonance

There is a psychological term for this phenomenon called cognitive dissonance. Cognitive dissonance is when what we believe is different than how we behave. One obvious example of this is when people smoke (their behavior) they know it can cause cancer and cardiovascular disease (thought). If a person has an affair, for example, he or she might justify cheating because of a neglectful spouse. The neglect (a lie) allows the person to justify his or her actions and still maintain a level of dignity. There are many times when we lie to ourselves.

Self-Deception

We lie to ourselves when we stake our happiness on one aspect of our lives. We might tell ourselves that we'll be happy when we meet our soulmate or when we buy our first home. But even if we meet our soulmate and buy our first home, we are never satisfied with what we have. We always want more than what we have since biologically, to evolve and grow, we must strive for more. If we are simply satisfied with every goal that we reach, we won't evolve or strive.

You are lying to yourself when your emotions don't match your words. If someone hurt you or you were in an argument with someone, and you don't share how you feel, then you are in cognitive dissonance. By telling yourself how you feel and sharing those feelings with another person, you could resolve the current conflict and possible similar ones in the future.

When your behavior doesn't match your proclamations, then you are lying to yourself. Let's say that you proclaim to a co-worker that your immediate supervisor doesn't know what he's doing and that you could replace him in six months. If, after making that statement, you do nothing to improve your skills, take on new projects, etc. then your behavior does not match your proclamation. Your words were just a passing statement made to entertain a co-worker.

You lie to yourself when you blame the time for your lack of success. By saying that you can't fulfill your dreams because you don't have enough time simply means your dream isn't important enough for you. Even if you work 40-hours a week at a job, there are still nights and weekends to work on your dream. People "binge-watch" TV Series on Netflix or Hulu for as much as 4-7 hours at a time, and blame the time for their failures. Blaming the lack of time for not pursuing your dreams is self - deception. You are telling yourself that you don't want to achieve your goal. You place the value on what's important. If your screenplay, your acting career, your mountain climbing were important, you would find the time.

You lie to yourself when you make extreme statements and exaggerations to avoid doing something. For example, you might say there are no good work opportunities out there—nothing, nada—no good jobs. You are lying to yourself because your statement can easily be disproven. Even in a tight job market, there are always opportunities to find work that you are skilled at or start a business that you believe in. By making these extreme statements, you are hiding behind your insecurities. As long as you continue to make irrational exaggerations about the way you see life, then you don't have to take any action. If you say, "I will never find my soulmate," you are committing to this notion so you can stay single even though you know you are wrong. Out of 7.5 Billion people in the world, can you honestly say that there is no one who is right for you? You are avoiding commitment because you choose to be alone.

If you exaggerate your abilities, you are lying to yourself. Because of our pride, our title, our status or position, we often tell others that we know what we're doing. When you tell others, "I got this," and you don't ask others for help on projects that you know that you can't do. Still, you only said that to make yourself look good. If you continue to exaggerate your abilities, you will find yourself in situations that you can't handle, or you can't deliver on your promises. Be honest about your abilities. If you continue to exaggerate your abilities, you might hurt others if you make mistakes.

If you are never open to feedback from others, you are lying to yourself. What you're saying is your opinion is the only one that matters and the only one which should be considered. Once you learn to accept feedback from other people, you can learn from them and realize that someone else's opinion counts as much as yours does. Accepting feedback from other people could lead to successful collaboration with other people and perhaps better outcomes for the projects you are currently working on.

Lastly, if you feel that you are never wrong, you are lying to yourself. Even when a negative outcome is obviously your fault, you refuse to hold yourself accountable for your actions. By never assuming accountability for your actions, you are lying to yourself. For example, if your business fails, you might blame your partner. If your relationship fails, you might blame your boyfriend or girlfriend. If you continue to live your life this way you will never learn from your mistakes. If you feel that you are never wrong, you will keep on blaming other people for your mistakes. Accept responsibility for your actions. When you are wrong, say so and learn from the experience.

Action Steps

1. If you have two slices of cheesecake for desert although you want to lose weight, are you lying to yourself?
2. Do you practice self-integrity? Make a list of all the things you plan to do this week and complete every one.
3. Do you think our business leaders and government officials are people of integrity? Why or why not? Can you offer some examples of leaders who have or had self-integrity?

RESILIENCE

In his book, *Man's Search for Meaning*, Victor Frankl wrote: "Everything can be taken from a man but one thing: the last of human freedoms—to choose one's attitude in any given set of circumstances, to choose one's own way." Victor Frankl chronicled his experiences as a concentration camp inmate and slave laborer in Dachau in 1944. The psychiatrist from Vienna believed that we could find meaning in all forms of human existence and even in the harshest of circumstances when we feel that we are losing our very purpose for living.

Throughout his book, Frankl shows how human beings can be resilient in spite of adverse living conditions, trauma or tragedy. Resilience is the process by which we adapt during times of stress, such as job loss, health problems, the death of a loved one, relationship failures, custody battles and other traumas and tragedies such as natural disasters, terrorist threats or shootings. Resilience also counts in finding your way through depression and low points in your career such as periods of failure. If you have a resilient personality or disposition, you are better able to maintain your composure and a healthy level of physical and psychological wellness in the face of life's challenges.

Frankl wrote that even during periods of terrible conditions and psychic and physical stress man can still find spiritual freedom and the ability to choose to have a positive attitude despite all of the death, devastation, and horrors which the inmates were faced with every day of their captivity. Everything was taken away from a concentration camp inmate: their clothing, possessions, money, documents, jewelry, books, memorabilia, writing materials, and manuscripts. The concentration camp inmates had no physical proof to connect them to their lives. They were each given a number which was tattooed on their arm to serve as their only proof of identity. Despite all of this, they had the opportunity to choose, to decide whether or not to maintain one's dignity and composure in the face of the inhumanity and degeneration

ASK FOR MORE

which the inmates were forced to endure every day. One can maintain one's dignity in spite of being in a concentration camp.

How man endures his fate and the suffering he is forced to take, Frankl says, is how he finds meaning in his life. Faced with pain and suffering, he must use these opportunities to improve his moral values or succumb to them and lose all dignity as if he were an animal. Life has meaning for those who believe in a future for themselves. These were the people who believed that after their experiences in the camp they might be united with loved ones or they would be able to finish a creative work, unique to them.

If we are to find meaning in life such as the opportunity to raise a family, build a business or create art or literature, then we could find meaning in suffering. Every individual has a unique purpose in life. Once we know what our responsibility is in life, such as a loved one or a child who needs our care and attention, we cannot escape it. Once we know the why for our existence, we can find our how. Once liberated from three years in various concentration camps, Frankl returned to Vienna and helped people overcome painful experiences through his Institute of Logotherapy. Logotherapy means finding meaning in life.

RICHARD BELLMAN

Nelson Mandela was imprisoned for 27 years because he was found guilty of conspiracy to overthrow the South African government. Mandela and eight other National African Congress leaders wanted to put an end to apartheid, which denied basic human rights to black South Africans. Throughout his life, Mandela fought for equal rights and freedoms for all South Africans.

"I have cherished the ideal of a democratic and free society in which all persons will live together in harmony and with equal opportunities. It is an ideal for which I hope to live for and to see realized. But my Lord, if it needs be, it is an ideal for which I am prepared to die."

Nelson Mandela, Rivonia Trial, 1963

Nelson Mandela proved his commitment to the ideal of racial equality by never wavering from his firm stand against Apartheid. He was found guilty of conspiracy and sabotage and imprisoned for 27 years. Mandela proved his resilience by surviving the ordeal and went on to become the first black president of South Africa and a winner of the Nobel Prize. He proved to be the epitome of resilience. He always maintained his composure and gentle manner. He was always optimistic that he would bring about change in South Africa. He persevered in his mission to bring racial and social equality to South Africa. He lived by his words: "There is no passion to be found in playing small—in settling for a life that is less than the one you are capable of living." He was a firm believer in fulfilling one's potential. The feeling that there is always more to our lives than what we're currently manifesting is what causes us anxiety and frustration.

Mandela believed that during times of distress we could propel ourselves forward to develop our real strengths and overcome any trauma or distress which we're enduring. Whatever interests that you have been keeping inside of you, it's time to give your dreams life and take action towards achieving them. Nelson Mandela was released from prison in 1990 and went on to become the first post-Apartheid president of South Africa on May 9, 1990.

Another example of an individual who has proved to be extremely resilient despite a major physical handicap is the actor turned activist, Christopher Reeve (1952-2004). Best known for his role as Superman, Reeve suffered a horse-riding accident in 1995 that left him paralyzed from the neck down. For the last ten years of his life, Reeves vowed that he would be able to walk by his 50th birthday in 2002. He dedicated his entire life to his recovery and physical therapy.

RICHARD BELLMAN

Christopher Reeve became an outspoken advocate for stem cell research. Stem cells have the ability to develop into any type of tissue, which could improve the condition of patients who suffer from Parkinson's disease; Alzheimer's disease and spinal cord injuries. Reeve took his cause to the United Nations and to radio and TV announcers who would hear his plea. Reeves who used his vast resources from acting to help his recovery, also used his name and recognition to promote the stem cell research cause which could help millions of patients once the research into stem cell research is conclusive and the methods can be successfully applied for treatment.

People who display resilience upon recovering from traumatic events have realistic plans for their future and take steps towards carrying them out. They take the very cause which has hurt them and grow from their experience to help others in the same set of circumstances. They have a positive self- image and display confidence in their strengths. Resilient people are problems solvers and gifted communicators. They can keep their emotions in check in spite of suffering emotional and financial losses.

According to the American Psychological Association, factors which influence resilience are good relationships, positive outlooks, and goal setting. Good relationships are crucial to growing and enhancing one's resiliency. Good relationships with family members and friends are critical in creating a network which can help you when things get difficult. Being active in civic groups and faith-based organizations can also help to give one a sense of security and protection.

Changing your response to events and situations can also build resiliency. Once a stressful event happens in your life, you cannot change it, but what you can change is how you interpret and respond to the event. Your response and positive outlook will make all the difference in deciding the outcome.

Developing realistic goals that you can achieve and taking action towards working towards them will help you to build resilience. As you complete small goals, your confidence level will increase, and you will be better equipped to come out of any negative experience with a positive and resilient attitude.

Action Steps

1. How can resilience help in dealing with failure as you try to accomplish your goals?
2. Think of a negative experience that you got through. Did it help to have family members and friends at your side?
3. How can you think of other ways to develop resilience?

Ask For
Health

16 Weight

Now and then, the media, TV, radio and newspapers will broadcast something "new" regarding obesity and weight gain in the United States. Two reports published by the Center for Disease Control and Prevention in June of 2016 revealed that 38% of U.S. adults are obese, including 17% of teenagers. In other words, these people have a BMI of more than 30. If a person has a BMI of 25 or more, then that person is overweight. One-third of Americans fall into this category. Put simply, almost two-thirds of the country is overweight or obese.

RICHARD BELLMAN

Body mass index is a unit of measurement of body fat based on height. Since the BMI is not gender based, it is pretty simple to see what a healthy BMI is. A BMI measurement of 18.5 is considered underweight or malnourished; a BMI of 18.5 to 25 is considered a healthy weight, while a BMI of 25-30 is considered overweight and a BMI of 30 or over is considered obese. The Body Mass Index formula was developed by Lambert Quartelet, a Belgian astronomer, and mathematician in the 1830's. The formula is formed by dividing your weight in kilograms by your height in meters squared.

Obesity has been linked to several medical risks including Hypertension, Coronary Heart Disease, Type 2 Diabetes, Stroke, Asthma, and Arthritis. Since more people are overweight or obese, these health risks add to the burden of health costs for everyone. Indirect costs of obesity include productivity costs or the rising economic costs because of the increase of obesity in the workplace. Obesity as a condition also leads to higher incidences of disability and increased premiums for insurance applicants who are obese based on their increased risk. Premature mortality is also connected to obesity, as experts have controlled for other factors related to longevity such as smoking. Obesity also adds to the cost of health insurance and life insurance premiums, making it more expensive for the general population.

ASK FOR MORE

Despite all of these proven scientific risks, being overweight and obesity has become the new normal in the United States. The average American weighs almost 23 pounds above his or her normal body weight. Many children and adults don't consider themselves overweight since everyone looks the same. There is more acceptance of the heavier body type since more people have them. In 2016, plus size model Ashley Graham joined several other plus size models on the runway at New York Fashion week. The fashion industry, in general, realized that clothing sales were being affected by models who were sizes 2-4, most women couldn't see themselves wearing clothes worn by a woman that size. The trend toward plus sizes for women is technically off the runway and in women's closets around the country. Acceptance of plus size means that women don't have to starve themselves to be fashionable.

In a country where free choice and easy availability of food is common, irresponsible eating habits are common. Major League Eating, an organization that promotes eating contests and events around the country, encourages contestants to consume large quantities of unhealthy foods in record times. One competitive eater holds the record for eating 8.31 pounds of Armour Vienna Sausage in 10 minutes. Another competitive eater finished off 182 strips of Smithfield bacon in 5 minutes. All competitions must first be sanctioned by the MLE, which checks for safe eating conditions and I would also hope sanitary conditions and food safety.

We are a fast food nation, loyal (and addicted) to the easy button. Americans love to eat out because it's easy, usually safe and relatively cheap. The fast food industry is a $570 billion industry globally, with $200 billion generated right here in the United States. There are over 200,000 fast food restaurants in the United States. On average, 50 million Americans eat at one or more of them every single day. These numbers alone are staggering. It would take a statistician to count the number of actual calories consumed by all of these diners who are supporting the growth of their waistlines along with the growth of the economy.

While many fast food companies such as McDonald's and Dominos are offering healthier choices such as salads on their menus, most people are conditioned to order the unhealthy choices they are conditioned to enjoying. Will it help if you have a chef salad before you bite into a Big Mac? Will having an Asian Chicken salad leave you with enough "room" in your stomach for three slices of pepperoni pizza?

Other factors have led to the obesity epidemic in the United States. In *Fat Land*, Greg Critser cites the imbalance between caloric intake and physical activity leads to

ASK FOR MORE

obesity. Critser claims the imbalance was due to government incentives to increase corn production during the Nixon administration in 1971 which coincided with the Japanese invention of high fructose corn syrup. Soon after, high fructose corn syrup was infused as a sweetener into Twinkies, cookies, pastries and soda.

In this same period, between 1970 and 1980, fast food restaurants such as McDonald's introduced the concept of value meals which included a hamburger, French fries, and soda, instead of selling these items a la carte. McDonald's also came up with the idea of "supersizing" meals, which is offering diners more food through larger sizes for a little extra money. More people ate out over the span of two decades, between 1970 and 1990, which translated into eating more. Also, public schools began to accept corporate sponsors such as soda companies and fast food chains whose intention was to turn them into customers after school and once they were through with the K-12 school system.

The documentary, *Fed Up* blames the obesity epidemic on sugar in our food supply. It cites evidence as to how 80% of the 600,000 food products in the United States have added sugar. Nutritionists believe that sugar is as addictive as cocaine. Dr. Robert Lustig, author of *Fat Chance* also believes that sugar is a culprit for weight gain that should be avoided at all costs. The film suggests that viewers take the 10-day no sugar challenge, which includes juices and processed foods such as crackers.

While there are many different reasons for obesity in the United States, solutions to the overall problem depend on personal accountability. In his 2009 book, *Food Rules: An Eater's Manual*, investigative journalist Michael Pollan takes issue with the Western diet, what we eat and how we eat. The result is a small but concise book of simple rules that one can follow to improve one's health by improving one's diet. These rules include basic tenets such as:

Rule #6: Avoid food products that contain more than five ingredients (because of added preservatives, sweeteners, sugar and salt all must be counted as ingredients.)

Rule #12: Shop the peripheries of the supermarket and stay out of the middle. (Most processed foods, such as cookies, crackers and cereals, frozen foods, energy drinks and sodas are all located in the middle.)

Rule #20: It's not food if it arrived through the window of your car (There's no explanation provided in the book either!)

Dr. Brian Wansink, a food psychologist, also advocates personal choice and accountability when it comes to what we put in our mouths. In his book, *Mindless Eating*, Wansink describes ways that we could be more mindful of what and how we eat our food. Dr. Wansink makes the following simple suggestions:

- Taking less to eat than you think you want: by taking 20% less food, you will eat less, offer 20% more vegetables.
- Serve your food on smaller plates; this will help you to eat less.
- Keep serving dishes out of reach after you have taken a portion; this will make overeating inconvenient.
- Eat slow and without any distractions such as a TV, or looking at a cell phone.

Weight gain and obesity are, of course, tied to personal accountability. By changing our eating habits, we will be able to eat less food and avoid overeating which can lead to weight gain and obesity. No one is forcing us to pull into the McDonald's drive through every day. We choose what we want to eat and make 200 food choices every day, according to Dr. Wansink. Out of those 200 choices we should be able to decide on foods that keep us healthy: plants, vegetables, fruits and grains that are most invigorating for us regarding nutrition and over the long run, the best investment for our being here for a long time.

Action Steps

1. Habits are usually formed over 21 days. Keep a food journal for 21 days and notice how you will consciously avoid sweets and baked items such as cookies and bread because you may not want to list them with other healthy foods. Keeping a food journal is an easy way to lose 5-8 pounds in 21 days.
2. Try following the "periphery rule" by only shopping along the peripheries of your favorite grocery store. Do you notice what is different? Which items are missing from your standard list?
3. Try avoiding eating out for 21 days. Which restaurants are hardest to resist? Which foods can you make at home that would probably be healthier for you?

17 Exercise

The adage has always been if you want to lose weight, then diet and exercise! Exercise can, of course, influence weight loss. The problem is we eat too much of the wrong foods, and we don't exercise enough to maintain a healthy weight. After surveying 450,000 people by asking them how often they engaged in an aerobic physical activity and for how long, 80% of respondents said that they don't get the recommended amounts of exercise each week.

The U.S. Government recommends that adults get at least 2½ hours or 150 minutes of moderate-intense aerobic exercise or 1½ hours or 90 minutes of vigorous activity or a combination of both. The CDC also recommends muscle-strengthening activities such as weight-lifting, push-ups, and sit-ups.

To underscore these findings, the latest reports on sitting and sedentary behavior show how damaging physical inactivity can be damaging to overall health and longevity. Sedentary behavior can lead to cardiovascular disease, cancer, and Type 2 Diabetes. According to the World Health Organization, physical inactivity is the fourth leading risk factor for death around the world, linked to 5 million deaths. Prolonged sitting, for sometimes 8-12 hours a day can increase the risk of contracting Type 2 Diabetes by 90%.

Regular exercise, on the other hand, has many health benefits for individuals who maintain a regular exercise routine. The health benefits of exercise include:

- Lower body weight,
- Lower blood pressure (systolic and diastolic)
- Control of blood sugar and cholesterol
- Lowered cardiovascular disease
- Lowered risk of stroke
- Strengthened bones through weight training
- Reduced incidences of cancer
- Fewer infections; less fatigue
- Better moods through endorphins and dopamine which are released in high impact exercise

ASK FOR MORE

- Less depression
- Improved sleep
- Increased longevity

Many people believe that lack of physical activity is due to modern living and technology. Cars in densely populated urban areas have largely replaced walking and biking, especially as more people have moved away from urban centers to the suburbs. Elevators and escalators have replaced stairs. Dishwashers have replaced doing dishes by hand. Computer technology has replaced manual labor. Robots have replaced assembly line work in manufacturing. Many affordable snow blowers and ride on lawnmowers have replaced shoveling snow and mowing lawns. TV and video games have all but replaced outdoor physical activities for both children and adults. A now popular gadget is called the Roomba, a robotic vacuum that users can turn on and wait until the machine covers an entire span of floor, carpet or tile before turning itself off. Moving walkways abound at major airports in the United States and around the world.

The R.W. Rogers Company manufactures and sells motorized handicap carts which boast of a 500-pound rider capacity and a 150-pound basket capacity. These carts are readily available in front of the store and very easy to use. They, of course, diminish the activity that one would benefit from by at least walking through the store to select healthy food choices.

Despite all of these conveniences, it is still relatively easy to get your best mix of cardio and strength training. Here, we'll look at activities that fall into each category. Cardio training includes walking which improves memory; well-being, heart health and stimulates creativity. Cycling is known to increase brain connectivity and improve depression. Running improves bone density and strength and increases longevity.

For strength, try Yoga. Yoga involves lifting one's weight through flexed poses and arching techniques. It also involves strength building through stretching of muscles and reduces stress. Weight training may conjure images of big guys on muscle beach, but anyone can weight train. By using a pair of weights, 10-20 pound dumb bells will strengthen bone and muscle at any age or gender. Resistance bands are also effective and easier to carry when traveling or using at the office. Tai chi involves slow, gentle movements. The poses strengthen the back, abdomen and both upper and lower body. The practice is also a great pain reliever.

Simple practices such as standing longer will reduce the risk of cancer and debilitating diseases. Gardening, including planting, raking, watering grass and in the winter months, shoveling counts as physical activity. Housework such as vacuuming, making beds, doing dishes manually while standing, moving furniture, and dusting also counts as physical activity. Other tricks for getting more physical activity into your day, is to park farther away from the store where you plan to shop. Take the stairs instead of using the elevator at the office. When possible, instead of hiring someone to do your housework, do it yourself. Physically take someone in another department a document instead of emailing it. Many socially responsible companies are looking for ways to introduce employee wellness programs into work activities because studies show that a healthier payroll will increase profits.

Up to 60% of U.S. companies offer wellness programs. Wellness programs are known to reduce healthcare costs, improve employee health and productivity; reduce absenteeism; lower stress levels; higher employee retention rates; fewer reported sick days; lower insurance premiums; higher self-esteem; increased energy and morale; better attitudes; and greater interest to succeed.

Many of the country's large corporation have adopted wellness programs that include fitness activities to promote employee health.

- Online retailer Zappos offers its employees a variety of fitness perks including gym memberships; free fitness classes; nap rooms and reimbursement for running marathons. The company employees a full-time fitness coordinator who schedules "Wellness Adventures" and has employees participate in physical activities such as golf lessons, laser tag, trampolining, and basketball games.

- Exxon-Mobil has a North Houston complex that includes volleyball games and a fitness center. The Globalfit Discount Program allows employees and retirees to join popular health clubs at discounted rates.
- Chevron has instituted a company-wide "Get Moving" policy that encourages employees to "Make physical activity a part of your day." Voluntary participation in the wellness program makes employees eligible for monetary contributions to their Health Care Spending Account. The company also provides employees fitness centers.
- Fitbit, a company which makes digital fitness trackers practices what it preaches. It encourages other companies to use their devices called "Fitbit Wellness Programs" to incentivize employees to participate in step competitions for better health. Fitbit participates in "Workout Wednesdays" where employees can join workout programs throughout the day and also has quarterly step challenges, where employees compete against one another to see who has achieved the most steps.

ASK FOR MORE

Just like many U.S. corporations are becoming increasingly socially responsible by improving fitness and wellness programs for its employees, Federal, state, and city governments are also doing their part to make fitness a habit for Americans regardless of their age, status or gender. The President's Council on Fitness, Sports and Nutrition produces public service announcements regarding the benefits of physical activity for children on television and radio. Former First Lady, Michelle Obama, created the "Let's Move" program which serves as a platform to create wellness programs at the elementary and high school level that combines healthy nutrition and physical fitness. Many cities around the country have instituted programs that encourage physical fitness through increased expansion of bike paths and bicycle rentals for riders to use to explore different parts of the city.

- Capital Bikeshare is a service in the Washington, DC area where tourists can find a bicycle for rent at any number of stations located throughout the city, rent for a short trip, rent for the day, or rent by the year.
- Critical Mass is an organized bicycle riding event held in select cities throughout the country. Known as America's Largest Community Bicycle Ride, the event is held on the last Friday night of every month and usually meets downtown. The

event began in San Francisco in the late 1990's, and there are now Critical Mass rides around the world.
- Boulder, Colorado is a great place to work out if you are so inclined to work there. There are 20 fitness centers for every 100,000 people, so this is why only 15% of the city's adults are obese as opposed to the 27% national average.

While these programs are impressive, exercise takes willpower and motivation. Start by finding the time to exercise and start off slow. Get up 30 minutes earlier than usual and start walking outside, weather permitting. Skip one hour of television every day and walk during that time instead. Join a gym and commit to going to the gym 2-3 times a week for six weeks until it begins a habit. Exercise throughout the day by doing push-ups, sit-ups, and stretches in your office or cubicle. Use lunch time for walking around the campus, or walking to a local eatery where you pick up a salad to eat when you return to the office. Find a workout companion at work or in your building who would like to also exercise with you on a regular basis. Get moving and start reaping the benefits of regular exercise!

ASK FOR MORE

Action Steps

1. Start training for a 5KM race, Check out the website: www.raceplace.com and look for a fun 5KM race in your local area.
2. Check out your company's wellness plan? Have you been participating? Will you help to create one if there isn't one in place?
3. Does your building have a gym or fitness center that you haven't been using? Check it out!
4. Take a free tour of your local fitness center and consider joining!

18 Sleep

So far, I have recommended that you ask for more and live out your lifelong dream with determination and commitment. It may sound counterintuitive, but to you maintain peak performance and optimal health, you will need to get more rest and adequate sleep every night. Sleep deprivation could have devastating effects on our health and safety. The benefits of adequate sleep are in fact crucial to mental and physical health including work productivity, immune system, weight loss, creativity, vitality, and heart and brain health.

The reason we sleep is to regenerate important bodily functions. During the day, our brains take in a vast amount of information and sleep allows us to consolidate the information we need into our memory. The facts that we uncover and our experiences need to be transferred from short term memory to long term memory. Studies have shown that people who get adequate sleep tend to retain information better and later perform better on tasks which require memory retrievals, such as examinations and quizzes. Our bodies need sleep to rejuvenate and grow muscle, repair tissue and synthesize hormones. Sleep is crucial for controlling weight since when you lose sleep, stress hormones known as cortisol levels rise. Cortisol activates reward centers in the brain that make you want more food, while the lack of sleep also lowers levels of leptin in the body that signal satiety. If you get up tired, you will feel hungrier than normal throughout the day; this could lead to excessive weight gain over time.

Sleep needs vary by age. Newborns require the most sleep to grow and develop, 14-17 hours a day. Adults require 7-9 hours of sleep every day. Deep restorative sleep is dependent upon several factors:

- Avoiding alcohol at least two hours before bedtime
- Avoiding nicotine throughout the day

- Reducing exercise activity at least 3-4 hours before going to sleep
- Avoiding blue light by looking at cell phones and tablets at least two hours before going to sleep

Signs of sleep deprivation may include needing an alarm clock to get up, having difficulty getting out of bed, sluggishness, and fatigue in the late afternoon, falling asleep in meetings; feeling drowsy after meals, and feeling like taking a nap throughout the day. Sleep deprivation can ruin your health and your outlook.

The Effects of Sleep Deprivation

- Fatigue
- Lack of motivation
- Depression
- Irritability
- Moodiness
- Decreased sex drive
- Poor concentration
- Memory problems
- Reduced creativity
- Muddled thinking
- Impaired judgement
- Weakened immune system
- Colds
- Infections
- Weight gain

- Delirium
- Hallucinations
- Nervous breakdown

Sleep deprivation has caused accidents which have affected public safety. Most recently, on December 1, 2013, Metro-North engineer William Rockefeller fell asleep at the controls of the speeding train and derailed the train, killing four people and injuring several dozens of passengers who were commuting to work. Although the speed limit on the curve was posted as 30 miles per hour, the train was going 82 miles per hour as Rockefeller fell asleep. Other disasters which were caused due to sleep deprivation include:

- The Chernobyl Nuclear Power Plant disaster affected 240 people with radiation poisoning and 28 deaths within the first few weeks of the spill. The engineers who were working at the plant at the time had been working shifts of 13 hours or more.
- The Challenger Space Shuttle exploded just seconds after its January 1986 launch killing all seven of the crew members onboard. Managers who were working on the launch had only two hours of sleep before arriving to work at 1 a.m. on the morning of the launch.

ASK FOR MORE

- In 1989, the Exxon Valdez Oil Spill was due to a supertanker running aground, causing 258,000 barrels of crude oil to spill into Prince William Sound in the Gulf of Alaska. Third mate Gregory Cousins was sleeping at the helm of the ship, so he was unable to turn the ship around and avert the disaster. The entire crew had worked 22 hours loading oil onto the ship.
- American Airlines Flight 420 overshot the airport runway at Little Rock International Airport on June 1, 1989, killing 11 people which included the captain and injured the first officer and 105 passengers and other crew members. The National Transportation Safety Board (NTSB) ruled the cause of the accident due to "impaired performance due to fatigue."

Long shifts that result in sleep deprivation have drastic consequences on the country's highways. The National Sleep Foundation survey showed that 60% of drivers, 168 million drivers had driven a vehicle feeling drowsy, and 103 million have fallen asleep at the wheel. Over 100, 000 police-reported crashes are related to driver's nodding off while driving. Sleep deprivation also affects our mood, our ability to focus and concentrate and use optimal mental performance. Not sleeping enough can also lead to irritability, mood swings, and depression.

When people don't get enough sleep, their learning and memory can also be affected. Sleep helps learning and memory because, through sleep, the brain consolidates new information that was learned throughout the day. Children and students who cram before an exam will do poorly on examinations the next day because they are unable to retain enough information to recall everything they need to know. Sleep deprivation also affects our ability to focus and concentrate on tasks, especially those that involve solving problems.

Lack of sleep affects people's short term health. Healthy subjects in studies were deprived of sleep for short terms and results showed changes to the body which can be linked to diseases over the long term. The effects included increased levels of stress; higher blood pressure; impaired glucose control and inflammation. Lesser known effects of sleep deprivation include the prevalence of alcohol use among sleep-deprived since alcohol first acts as a sedative when consumed but drinkers react to it later and have trouble sleeping. Life expectancy can be reduced by 15% by sleeping less than 5 hours a night.

In *Rest: Why You Get More Done When You Work Less*, author Alex-Soojung-Kim Pang makes the argument that productivity at work is not based solely on the number of hours worked. In the long run, overworking can hurt productivity. The author also states that work in-

ASK FOR MORE

volves creativity and critical thinking more than we might realize. Once we rest, we are better able to use our innovation and problem-solving skills to accomplish more at work.

Soojung-Kim Pang makes the argument that human sleep may have helped shape human civilization itself. Evolutionary biologists David Samson and Charles Nunn believe that short sleep allowed humans to defend themselves against nocturnal dangers and let them gather food and care for the young during daylight hours. Longer sleep, on the other hand, proved to be enough to consolidate memories, regenerate muscles and tissues in the body, repair any damaged cells and clear out toxins in the brain; this led to early humans developing stronger cognitive abilities.

In his study of the sleep patterns of baboons and orangutans, Dr. Samson noticed that while baboons sit up while they sleep, orangutans like to get into bed, nestle into a comfortable prone sleeping position and slumber away. Modern humans are more like the orangutan than the baboon. We like sleeping lying down.

In the First Class section of a 5-hour Delta Airlines flight from Richmond, Virginia to Los Angeles, California, I was seated in a pod that reclined all the way down. The seats looked like pods, side by side, two on the left side of the plane, two in the middle, and two on the right side of the plane.

While many major airlines accommodate their Premier and First Class passengers with reclining seats that can turn into beds on long flights, airplane passengers do their best to get some shut eye while up in the air. Some suggestions to get some sleep on a long flight are: taking a window seat where you won't be disturbed; using a neck pillow; covering up with a blanket; and listening to relaxing music. In between flights, many major international airports now offer sleeping accommodations for travel-weary passengers. These structures range from pod-like to cubes and allow passengers to sleep for fees which range from $15–$25 an hour depending on the size of the accommodations and the amenities which may include bathroom and sink, and Wi-Fi.

Some major U.S. companies who are socially responsible allow their employees to sleep on the job. Every year lost productivity costs the U.S. economy $63 Billion because of employees who don't get enough sleep. Companies, therefore, encourage brief twenty to twenty-five minute naps so that employees can recharge their energy levels and get back to work more focused and energized. Companies now encourage napping on the job and willingly provide "quiet rooms" or "nap rooms" where employees can go to meditate, do yoga or sleep. Zappos, the online shoe retailer, offers employees lounges that include bean bags, recliners, and a couch at their Las Vegas, Nevada headquarters. Nike offers its employees quiet rooms at their headquarters in Portland, Oregon and Google offers its employees nap pods, shower rooms, and coffee bars to engage them at their Mountain View, CA headquarters.

So, sleep just makes good sense for all of us for our overall health, both physical and mental. Sleep allows us to focus on the task at hand while eliminating distractions. Sleep allows us to retain more information by improving our memory, learning, and outcomes on examinations. Sleep allows us to regulate hormones that could lead to weight gain, cardiovascular disease, and stroke. By getting enough sleep, we can control our moods and be less irritable. So if you want to make a difference in your life and contribute something of lasting value to the world, don't rush the process. Getting less sleep by being more productive is not the answer. Get more sleep and complete more quality work that will have lasting value.

Action Steps

1. Go to www.sleep.org, a website of sleep resources affiliated with the National Sleep Foundation and take the sleeper quiz to find out what kind of sleeper you are.
2. Try going to sleep at the same time every night and waking up at the same time every day. Try to get 7-9 hours every night for a week and log your progress.
3. Do you use alarm clocks to get you up? Do you rely on the snooze button? Try getting 7-9 hours of sleep every night and keep your alarm at least 10 feet from the bed. Make a commitment to get up at the first alarm for seven days and track your progress.

Companionship and Health

There's an old joke that married men don't live longer than their bachelor buddies; it just feels longer! However, the truth is married men do live longer than single men. Married women rate themselves as healthier than their single counterparts while married men seem to have better immune systems because they report having far fewer colds or major illnesses than their bachelor counterparts. Married men are around half as likely to commit suicide as single men. Married people report less depression in their lives, and

40% of married people say they are satisfied with their lives compared to 25% of single people.

These findings formed the basis of *The Case for Marriage: Why Married People are Happier, Healthier and Better off Financially* by authors Linda Waite and Maggie Gallagher. In this chapter, I would like to show how companionship and long-term friendships are crucial to one's health and longevity and how social isolation and loneliness are detrimental to one's health. Waite and Gallagher contend through their book that married people are better off financially, live longer and are in better health, both mentally and physically. Living together doesn't count because people who cohabitate may have multiple partners and may not be completely committed to the safety and well-being of their partners in the same way married people are. You must get hitched and stay together for a while to reap the health benefits of marriage.

In a recent article in the AARP Bulletin, entitled *9 Ways Your Mate Can Affect Your Health*, author Candy Sagon compiled the various ways couples benefit from being together.

> *"A good marriage enhances health because having someone you love and want to keep around encourages healthy behavior."* Christine Proulx, Associate

ASK FOR MORE

Professor of Human Development and Family Science, University of Missouri

Studies have shown a firm connection between marriage and health. Marriage can indeed improve one's overall well-being and physical and mental health. As a couple ages together, over the span of decades they begin to mirror each other's emotional and physical health because of their interdependency. Studies have proven that similarities exist among longtime couples regarding their kidney function, cholesterol levels, grip strength, depression and overall difficulty performing daily tasks.

The adage, "In sickness and in health" actually does apply to longtime married couples. If one partner is suffering from depression, the other will feel his or her pain and attempt various ways to support or alleviate the stress or pain on behalf of the other. Even nagging, which on its surface is considered by many men to be annoying, has health benefits since many men will seek out medical treatment for a condition if prodded and improve their overall health or weight loss because their spouse is urging them to do so.

Furthermore, interdependency increased a couple's overall mental health and well-being. If one spouse considered him or herself to have a positive outlook on life, both partners experienced fewer chronic illnesses such as diabetes and arthritis. Conversely, frequent arguing between partners often leads to cardiovascular disease and elevated blood pressure for both partners.

Partners in a committed marriage were also shown to emulate each other's good habits. If one spouse exercises, the other will usually follow his or her example. In a recent John Hopkins University study it was found that when the wife began to exercise more, her husband was 70% more likely to follow suit and increase his activity as well. When the husband stepped up his exercise goals, his wife was 40% more likely to increase her activity as well. Similarly, if one spouse develops negative habits such as overeating, or drinking too much, their partners might also run the risk of developing unhealthy conditions such as pre-diabetes.

Aside from the health benefits of long-term companionship, the key to happiness in life is the strength of our social connections. The Harvard Grant Study followed 268 Harvard undergraduate men over the course of their lives. The study included in-depth surveys of their overall health, alcohol intake, relationships, career choices and income levels. The findings published in the book, *Triumphs of Experience* by Psychiatrist George Vaillant revealed an in-depth study of the human experience. Vaillant directed the study from 1972 to 2004. Vaillant writes that there are two pillars of happiness: "One is love. The other is finding a way of coping with life that does not push love away." Vaillant also said that connection in life is crucial to our feelings of satisfaction and joy. Strong relationships can bring life satisfaction. Connection to one's career regarding doing something which fulfills you and brings you meaning is more important than traditional notions of success such as money and status. Since the study took place over 75 years, Vaillant found that social ties are even more crucial to longevity, and reducing stress later in life. Couples in long-term relationships were happier, healthier and more successful.

Loneliness

Loneliness, on the other hand, now affects over 60 million Americans. It can become a serious health risk that adversely affects health just as much as obesity and smoking. Loneliness can increase one's risk of heart disease and stroke and also increase the risk of high blood pressure. Lonely people have an increased chance of developing dementia and are more prone to feelings of depression. University of Chicago professor John Cacioppo has studied the effects of loneliness on mental and physical health for over 21 years. In his book, *Loneliness: Human Nature and the Need for Social Connection*, Cacioppo states that loneliness evolved because it allowed our ancestors to depend on social connections for safety and successful reproduction. Early humans who banded together were more likely to survive by sharing resources and feeling better than by being alone and insecure. By being connected, we are less agitated and stressed than when we feel lonely. Feeling connected to someone may also lower feelings of depression and hostility. While our society values individualism and competition, values such as community and family must also exist alongside it. Social connections are vital to our overall well-being.

Friendships can be extremely beneficial to one's health. They can reduce feelings of loneliness and despair we are feelings since good friends allow us an outlet to discuss our feelings and provide us with mutual support and companionship. Friends can improve our self-esteem and make us feel positive about the projects and work we care engaged in. Being with friends can boost our self-confidence and self-worth. Friends can help us cope with trauma such as grief, job loss, divorce, or returning home from a military deployment. Friends, like spouses, can encourage you to pursue a healthy lifestyle such as exercising more and stop negative habits such as smoking or drinking excessively.

In our age of social networks having many connections doesn't equate to having long-lasting close relationships with people who will stop everything to hear us out, and listen to us. There are a precious few people we can trust—*really trust*—with our deepest darkest secrets. Having someone by your side to whom you could tell your deepest secrets is liberating. When someone knows you well enough to detect your moods and thoughts, it isn't an invasion of privacy or an affront to your true independence. In a long-term relationship, feeling of interdependence can develop and thrive over time. Our need for social connections can improve our lives and build communities where feelings of cooperation and interdependency help to build social cohesion, much like the way early man and woman lived.

Action Steps

1. How many confidants do you have? Do you have friends that you can share anything? Make a list of your closest friends.
2. Why do we sometimes avoid social connections? Do we choose to be alone?
3. Ready to meet new people who share your interests? Go to Meetup.com and choose an interesting activity that you want to do with other people.

Mindful Meditation and Health

In our pursuit to get things done, and engage in multitasking, we may forget the main goal that we are after. We are so busy working towards success that we forget the reason why we are doing something. Our lives become automatic; the pursuit of material things takes over our psyche and rules our motivation. By obsessing over past mistakes, and worrying about future, we fail to live in the present moment. However, accepting ourselves in the present moment and appreciating ourselves and who we are is one of the health benefits of mindful meditation.

Dr. Jon Kabat-Zin laid down the foundations of mindfulness in mainstream medicine in his groundbreaking book, *Wherever You Go, There You Are*. In this small book, Kabat-Zin describes mindful meditation as stopping or non-doing. In this age of automation, where all or most of our actions are mechanical and driven by our material goals and our ambition, mindful meditation means stopping and doing nothing. Meditation is a practice in which we sit, relax and focus on the breath. Meditation practice was originated in Buddhism, loosely defined as a conscious effort to change how the mind works. The Pali word for meditation is "Bhavana" or to grow or to develop.

Kabat-Zin contends that in Western thinking, we try to control consequences which happen to us and our problems weigh heavily upon us until we take action to relieve our pains, Mindfulness, on the other hand, is a journey of self-observation and introspection. Through mindfulness, we can increase our awareness of our actions and live our lives with purpose and intention. Kabat-Zin contends that by using concentration in your meditation practice, you can overcome fears and inhibitions that once ruled your subconscious and be able to take on those fears and resolve problems in a constructive fashion. Kabat-Zin argued for an attitudinal shift while beginning a mindful meditation practice. These attitudes include:

- Non-judging: Think of how you always try to influence, judge and react to experiences around you. Suspend judgment of what happens around you, and observe; this will give you clarity and peace of mind.
- Patience: Start practicing patience by observing everything around you in real time. Be present in the moment and enjoy the fullness of the experience.
- Trust: Develop trust in yourself and listen to your instincts when making decisions and dealing with others.
- Beginner's Mind: Look at the world through fresh eyes, appreciate nature, the city, your surroundings, people whom you haven't noticed before. Free yourself of expectations from your past and begin again.
- Non-striving: Mindful meditation is all about non-striving and not achieving anything. It is all about non-doing, staying true to yourself and observing what is happening to you during the present moment.
- Acceptance: Stay in the present moment and see things as they are and avoid resistance or trying to change situations, people, and circumstances.
- Letting go: By cultivating letting go of past misconceptions or present judgments of situations we can appreciate the present moment, without attachment or labels.

RICHARD BELLMAN

Meditation is a common practice that is being used by some professional athletes, actors and business professionals. The old stereotype of the hippie going to the mountaintop to seek enlightenment or the lost soul going on an expedition to Nepal to seek a higher truth and leave the world of Western capitalism behind are outdated myths. Meditation can be practiced by anyone who is willing to commit the time and concentration necessary to grow and to develop oneself, and one's consciousness.

Mindful meditation has been proven to improve concentration, focus, and memory. Dr. Fadel Zeidan, a researcher at the Wakeforest University School of Medicine, conducted an experiment that proved that meditation techniques could improve cognitive skills. The study involved 49 participants. Each person was randomly assigned to be in a certain group. One group received the meditation training for 20 minutes a day for four consecutive days while the other group listened to excerpts of J.R.R. Tolkein's *The Hobbit* being read aloud to them. Both groups received tests which asked about mood, memory, attention and vigilance before and after the experiment. Both groups scored equally on tests before the experiment, but the meditation group scored significantly higher than the reading group on cognitive skills, such as concentration and memory retention. Meditation can increase concentration and attention even if practiced for short periods at a time. It stands to reason that meditation for longer periods of time can increase cognition skills such as memory, focus, concentration and attention over the long term.

How to Begin Mindful Meditation

When you begin to practice mindful meditation, you may wonder how to begin. Meditation is a practice; this means it must be done on a daily basis and done consistently to reap the full benefits of sustained meditation. You may want to begin with just five minutes a day, and then begin to develop more time on top of that as you progress. As for when and where to meditate, a quiet place is ideal and one where you can have privacy, and you won't be disturbed. While many companies around the U.S. have quiet rooms where employees can exercise, nap or meditate, you may want to look for an empty office, stairwell, rooftop, business center or lobby area where you won't be disturbed long enough to conduct your meditation.

When you meditate, you could sit in a lotus position, cross-legged or sit upright on a chair, with your hands on your knees. If your mind wanders with thoughts and things you have to do throughout the day, bring your thoughts and energy back to your breath. While meditating, focus on the breaths you take as you meditate, and if outside, you can listen to the sounds you hear such as birds, traffic or the wind, all the while focusing your energy on your breath. You may not see benefits right away, and it is all right to miss a day if you get too busy. Be kind to yourself and remember that meditation is a practice that must be extended over long periods of time to reap the benefits.

Mindful meditation has been practiced for thousands of years. While it is known to have various cognitive benefits such as reduced stress, more focused attention, and increased concentration, meditation can also have positive physical effects on the body and lasting changes to the brain. Since the cells and neurons of the brain are constantly forming new connections in response to outside stimuli such as stressful situations, through meditation, we can change these connections. In doing so, we can learn new patterns and change behavior. Mindful meditation can reduce stress, anxiety, depression, improve eating disorders, and lower blood pressure and reduce the risk of heart disease and stroke.

Proven Benefits of Mindful Meditation:

- Neuroscientist Dr. Hedy Kober conducted a study on the effects of mindful meditation on pain. Study subjects were given a pain stimulus, a hot

feeling on their arms. It was found that study participants were able to control and reduce feelings of pain after the meditation exercise.
- Meditation can change the gray matter in the hippocampus region of the brain. Since the hippocampus is sensitive to cortisol, it can be negatively impacted by stress by shrinking. A group of 16 subjects who engaged in an eight-week Mindfulness Based Stress Reduction program increased their gray matter in the hippocampus region.
- Mindful meditation can reduce blood pressure in patients whose high blood pressure was not controlled by medication alone. The "relaxation response" was first implemented by cardiologist Herbert Benson, whereas patients were advised to sit still for 20-30 minutes and repeat a mantra. At the Massachusetts General Hospital, Benson encouraged his patients to watch their diet and exercise and, of course, take their medication without fail. Then he asked his patients to try the relaxation response. Out of the 60 patients who tried the relaxation response, 40 had lowered their blood pressure and reduced their dosage of medication. Relaxation forms nitrous oxide which opens up blood vessels and allows for easier flow of blood through the body.
- Decreased depression and anxiety can also be listed as one of the many benefits of mindful

meditation. In a 2014 research study at the John Hopkins University, subjects who practiced 30 minutes of meditation a day improved symptoms of anxiety and depression that was equal to antidepressants.

You can practice mindful meditation anywhere. In fact, meditation can be elicited through walking slowly through the supermarket aisles, or while waiting for the bus or subway, or waiting in line. Meditation can be made part of your everyday life. By consistently slowing down and being in the present moment whenever you can, you will reap the health benefits of meditation. Memories will become more vivid. It will be easier to regulate your moods and control your anger. You will increase your concentration and focus. You will be more appreciative of the life you are leading and be more mindful of the time you have left on your voyage called life.

ASK FOR MORE

Action Steps

1. Find a quiet area of your home. Sit cross-legged on the floor and set your phone alarm timer for five minutes. Breathe in for four beats, hold for four beats and exhale for four beats. Try that for one week.
2. Try being mindful as you do household chores such as washing dishes; vacuuming; sweeping; and shoveling snow. Notice the repetition of movements and their subtleties.
3. Wake up at sunrise for seven straight days and watch the sunrise. Jot down your thoughts and emotions in a log. Make it a habit!

Ask For More Education

21 Intelligence and Achievement

Intelligence is always a factor when it comes to academic achievement, but to what degree? What are other factors necessary for achievement and success in life? Is academic achievement an indicator of success in life? Intelligence is hard to define. It may have different meanings in different cultures and ages and different skill sets. What is intelligence? What influences intelligence and how can it be measured? The standard definition of intelligence is the ability to learn from experience, solve problems, and use knowledge to adapt to new experiences.

RICHARD BELLMAN

Alfred Binet (1857-1911) designed the first successful test of intelligence. Binet, a French psychologist, was commissioned by the French public schools to design a test which would determine which children were at risk of falling behind their peers academically, or what we now call grade-level competencies. Binet worked with his colleague, Theodore Simon (1872-1961) to see which children were having the most trouble and needed extra help.

Their objective was to test children's memory, attention, and problem-solving skills. They found that some children were able to answer questions that normally only older children were able to answer, while some children were only able to answer questions that younger children were able to answer. Binet discovered the concept of mental age or a basic measure of intelligence based on the total average abilities of children of a certain age. The mental age represented the level of performance associated with a certain chronological age.

He believed that intelligence could be raised with self-discipline, and practice, and hoped that his tests would improve education overall by identifying students who needed extra attention. Binet also feared that if children were labeled as far below their mental age, they would be perceived as lost causes, and their peers and teachers may give up on them.

ASK FOR MORE

At the time, there was no standard number to describe intelligence. You either performed at your mental age or you performed above or below it, William Stern (1871-1938) was responsible for creating the actual Intelligence Quotient or "IQ." The formula was one's mental age divided by one's chronological age multiplied by 100. For example, if a child was 6 and his mental age was also 6, his IQ would be 100. But if a 4-year-old had a mental age of 5, the child would have an IQ of 125. The IQ worked well for children who develop chronologically but didn't work well for adults.

While the IQ continued to be used as a measure of intelligence and for employment screenings, in 1983, Howard Gardner proposed a model of multiple intelligences in his book, *Frames of Mind: Theory of Multiple Intelligences.*

> *"Intelligence is a biopsychological potential to process information that can be activated in a cultural setting to solve problems or create products that are of value in a culture."* Howard Gardner

According to Gardner, These intelligences included: Verbal/Linguistic, Logical-Mathematical, Spatial/Visual, Bodily-Kinesthetic intelligence, Musical, Interpersonal (getting along with others), Intrapersonal (knowing yourself), and Naturalistic.

Proponents of the Multiple Intelligence Theory believe that people are well rounded and must be encouraged to use all of their intelligences in school and teachers are encouraged to introduce activities that speak to their students' multiple intelligences and capabilities.

John D. Mayer and Peter Salovey introduced the idea of Emotional Intelligence in 1994. The notion of emotional intelligence included the ability to identify your emotions and those of others. It included the ability to harness emotions and apply them to tasks such as thinking and solving problems. Emotional intelligence included the ability to regulate emotions and also be able to cheer someone up or calm someone down. Emotional intelligence began to be used as a better predictor of performance and achievement than IQ.

Daniel Goleman, in his 1995 book, *Emotional Intelligence* described EI as the ability to identify, use, understand and manage your emotions in positive ways. Emotional Intelligence is when you can recognize your emotions, those of others and draw people to you through emotional engagement and understanding. According to Goleman, IQ is a fixed unit of measure of intelligence that doesn't change; it is fixed at birth and is part of the neocortex (logical reasoning), while emotional intelligence—your ability to use emotions and cognitive reasoning—is flexible and is part of the limbic system. While IQ is a good indicator of academic success, EQ is a better indicator of success in the workplace. People with high EQ make for great leaders and team members because of their innate ability to connect, understand and empathize with others in the workplace. Goleman developed four core abilities:

- **Self-awareness**: The ability to recognize your emotions and how they affect your thoughts and behavior.
- **Self-Management**: The ability to control impulsive feelings and behaviors, manage your emotions in healthy ways, and take the initiative, follow through on commitments, and adapt to changing circumstances.
- **Social Awareness**: The ability to understand the emotions, needs, and concerns of other people, look for emotional cues, feel comfortable socially and know and appreciate the group dynamics in an organization.
- **Relationship Management**: The ability to develop and maintain good relationships, communicate clearly, inspire and influence others, work well in a team and manage conflict appropriately.

According to almost twenty years of research, emotional intelligence has been linked to performance at work. Emotional intelligence is the foundation of many critical skills, so it impacts your overall profile on the job. The Talent Smart Company tested for 33 separate work-related skills and found that:

- 90% of top performers are also high in EQ, while only 20% of low performers are high in EQ.
- People with a high degree of emotional intelligence make more than $29,000 more than people with low EQ.

To increase your emotional intelligence, you must increase your self-awareness and understand how other people see you. To be a leader and inspire positive change, you must learn how to control your emotions. Self-awareness is a mix of having good social skills and practicing empathy and understanding of others. By reading situations and understanding people, you will be better equipped to get more work done and achieve your main objectives through others. By improving relationships with people, you will foster more cooperation at work and achieve more together.

Action Steps

1. Take an IQ test at https://memorado.com/iqtest.
2. Take an EQ test at http://www.ihhp.com/free-eq-quiz/
3. Take a Mensa Workout: https://www.mensa.org/workout.php

22 Intelligence and How Learning Can Change the Brain

Yes, it is possible to increase your intelligence. While IQ is a measure that remains stable throughout life, intelligence may be increased through learning new things. When we seek out new things, we are creating new synaptic connections in the brain and learning is happening. Through learning, we increase the neural plasticity in the brain, whereas new connections are growing between neurons. The more we retain of what we learn, the longer we retain the connections. By constantly learning new things, we are preparing ourselves for more learning. By learning new things, we create dopamine in the brain which in turn stimulates neurogenesis, the creation of new neurons that prepares the brain for learning.

More Proven Ways to Boost Your Intelligence

Challenging yourself is another way to train your brain to get smart. A study lead by Richard Haier at the Mind Research Institute in Albuquerque, New Mexico wanted to find out if challenging people is a way to increase their intelligence. He had 26 adolescent girls play the computer puzzle game called Tetris for 30 minutes a day for three months. The game typically requires a wide array of cognitive skills. Those who practiced the game showed greater brain efficiency and displayed a thicker cortex than those who didn't practice. After the experiment, they remained skilled at the game, but the scientists noticed a drop in the cortical thickness. That means that they got better at the game as they were practicing, but once they stopped playing, they weren't challenging their brains anymore. Increasing your intelligence requires a certain sense of discomfort or pain that has to be solved by moving to the next level of understanding and achievement.

Creative thinking is another way to boost your overall intelligence; it involves thinking differently and changing

ASK FOR MORE

your outlook. Yale psychologist Robert Sternberg put this notion to the test. He wanted to understand why the SAT, the Scholastic Achievement Test was so difficult that it was screening out students who aside from scoring high on the test showed great promise and achievement as college students. The College Board, which creates and administers the SAT funded Sternberg's research. Dr. Sternberg believed that there is more to intelligence than English grammar and solving geometry. He believed that intelligence should also be measured by a range of other abilities. He called the test "The Rainbow Project" and had it evaluate creativity and problem solving rather than analytical skills. Instead of including multiple choice questions, Sternberg asked students to write captions for various cartoons or write stories with unusual titles such as "The Octopus's Sneakers." Through the Rainbow Project, Sternberg believes he can convince the College Board to adapt and change the SAT so that it includes questions that appeal to attracting more diverse groups of students to college since the old standard favors success from wealthier segments of society.

Government public service ads to visit United States national parks ask people to Unplug. By unplugging from technology: I-pads; video game consoles; tablets; cell phones; and other devices, we can appreciate the nature at our national parks. The same is true about keeping your brain sharp and in working order. When you are traveling in a new city, buy a map at a local gas station and use it to get around instead of using your GPS or cell phone.

Write a handwritten note to a colleague instead of an email. Use a dictionary for spelling errors instead of spell check systems on your computer. Use an actual thesaurus, i.e. a book, instead of using a computerized system of finding new words to express the same meaning. By using technology too much, we could be oversimplifying our lives and our brains to the point of atrophy. Our dependence on technology could be hurting our brains in that there are parts of it that we aren't using anymore.

Another way to expand your wealth of knowledge is through social networking with other like-minded people. Through social media platforms such as Twitter, Instagram, Linked-In, and Facebook, it is possible to pose questions to thousands of people at the same time. They all might have different perspectives on any number of issues. These ideas can be shared and interchanged in ways that were never before possible. By writing to, messaging and yes, actually speaking to people in your network you are opening yourself up to new opportunities for not only professional and personal growth, but cognitive growth as well. Through networking with other people, you will be gaining access to their new ideas, perspectives, and points of view. Learning is all about changing your perspective and finding solutions to challenging problems. Through information sharing and networking with other people, you are not only increasing your capabilities through sharing knowledge and ideas; you are creating a better network of professionals who will be there for you throughout your career.

John Medina, a developmental molecular biologist, affiliate professor of Bioengineering at the University of Washington School of Medicine and author of *Brain Rules: 12 Principles for Surviving and Thriving at Work, Home and School* believes that there are 12 rules that we must follow to preserve our brain's normal functioning for optimal performance.

1. **Exercise**: Two sessions of aerobic exercise reduces your overall risk of dementia by 50%. Since exercise moves blood to the brain, offering it glucose for energy and oxygen to absorb toxic electrons that are remaining.
2. **Survive**: The brain is a survival organ that allowed our ancestors to survive in an outdoor environment while always on the move. Keep solving problems and keep relating to and forming alliances with fellow human beings for optimal survival strength.
3. **Every brain is different**: Various regions of the brain develop at different rates in different people.

All brains are different, and our intelligence doesn't always appear on standardized tests such as the IQ test.

4. **Brains don't pay attention to boring things**: The brain can only talk and breathe at the same time. The brain can't multitask, although we would like to think that we are accomplishing more by doing many things at once. The brain can only pay attention and focus on one thing at a time.

5. **Repeat and try to remember**: The brain can only hold seven pieces of information for more than 30 seconds. That's why phone numbers have seven numbers but not more. So if you want to retain the information for an hour or two, you will have to keep repeating the information over and over again.

6. **Go long**: Enhance your long-term memory. Most memories are like Snapchat used to be: most memories disappear within minutes, but those that make it after that sensitive time zone strengthen over time. Long-term memory may be more reliable if we incorporate new information gradually and repeat it in spaced out periods to improve retention. This explains why it is always better to study a subject in small increments on a daily basis instead of cramming information the night before a big exam.

7. **Sleep on it**: Regular sleep improves thinking and normal brain functioning. Neurons of the brain are very active when you sleep, trying to encode and make sense of what you learned and what happened to you during the day. Sleep improves attention, memory, mood, reasoning and dexterity.
8. **Chillax**: Stressed out brains can't learn as well as relaxed brains. When the brain is under chronic stress, adrenaline creates tears in blood vessels which could lead to damage that can cause a stroke, or heart attack, while cortisol created during stress could hurt the hippocampus region, disabling your ability to learn.
9. **Senses bring out emotions**: By using all of your senses, sight, smell, sound, taste and hearing, memories will be more vivid and long-lasting. Students can learn better with words and pictures, and some prefer video based story-telling to narration without film.
10. **See**: Vision is the most dominant of senses. We remember images and pictures above text.
11. **Gender**: Male brains are different from female brains: Men tend to have a larger amygdala, the region of the brain associated with emotion. Women tend to use a different part of the amygdala region to remember all of the emotional details.
12. **Brains are explorers**: We learn through active observation, experiment and by forming our

conclusions. The brain is also malleable and plastic like, so we can create neurons and learn new things throughout our lives.

Alfred Binet, who designed the first prototype of the IQ, the intelligence quotient did so with the French public school children's ability to progress in mind. As I described earlier, the intelligence score was designed to see which children were not keeping up with the current curriculum so that new and different educational programs could be written to get them back in line with the rest of their class. He knew there were genetic differences in intellectual ability between the students, but believed that education, practice, and individual effort could change intelligence. As we will see in the next chapter, effort, training, practice and one's physical and mental abilities determine one's mindset to accomplish goals in life.

ASK FOR MORE

Action Steps

1. Try learning a new language. See how novelty, trying new things can inspire you in other areas of your life.
2. Take an old board game like Scrabble out of the closet and play a few games instead of watching movies. Watch how your vocabulary improves as you remember words from your long-term memory that you had no longer used.

Mindset

The the 1976 movie, *Rocky*, (Sylvester Stallone), plays the title role of Rocky Balboa. In one lesser known scene, Rocky is courting Adrian (Talia Shire) at an ice skating rink that is closed to the public. Rocky tells Adrian that his father told him that he wasn't born with much a brain, so he might as well start using his body to fight. Adrian laughed and said that her mother said the opposite: "You weren't born with much of a body, so you better develop your brain!" Right away, the two had something in common, a fixed mindset.

In her book, *Mindset*, Stanford psychologist Carol Dweck, Ph.D. identified two core mindsets or sets of beliefs in our approach to learning, accomplishments, and achievements. The fixed mindset represents the belief that one's abilities are fixed from birth, and one's personal success is predetermined. The growth mindset, on the other hand, represents the belief that a person's mental and physical skills could be enhanced and developed through sheer will, effort, learning, and perseverance.

Our mindsets tend to shape our perspectives of success and our perception of our worth, abilities, and expectations. We are constantly keeping track of our motives and emotions. The fixed mindset is all about judging. If a person with a fixed mindset fails, that means they must be a failure. They can't do anything else. They didn't make the grade. People with a growth mindset, however, don't judge themselves in the same way. They are all about learning and taking control of the situation. If they encounter a setback, they wonder how they can improve. They ask themselves: "What can be learned from a setback and how can I accomplish this goal better the next time?"

In her research, Dr. Dweck wanted to know the difference in people's response to their respective failures; some people believe they fail at certain tasks because they lack the ability or right skills to accomplish a certain task. They would take this attitude with them even in areas of their lives where they had shown promise or capability.

ASK FOR MORE

People who thought they hadn't tried hard enough, on the other hand, would become even more determined by setbacks, failures or missed opportunities to advance or get better at their chosen skill.

Dweck ran an experiment with elementary school children who were having a tough time with their math problems. When some children encountered problems that they couldn't solve they were so frustrated that they refused to tackle problems which they were able to solve earlier. They even stopped for several days until they recovered. The students were divided into two groups. The first group was told that they should persist with their work and keep on going. They persisted despite failures. The second group, the control group which received no encouragement, showed no improvement but continued to display a pattern of effort, failure, and then, slow recovery.

These findings meant that when we have a growth mindset we see our failures not as obstacles to our success, or to an eventual solution. We see obstacles as ways to learn and try new things to achieve the positive outcomes we want. Students with a fixed mindset believe that their performance at the task is the most important thing. When you believe that people are judging you on your performance at a task, it can become a challenge to your self-image. Any setback or failure can become a threat.

For those with a fixed mindset, learning and growth are by-products. They typically only pursue activities which they know they're good at, without taking risks to learn and experience real growth. Students with learning goals, on the other hand, take those risks because they don't see failures as personal defeats but as opportunities to learn how they can improve on themselves.

At the beginning of the book, Dr. Dweck displays the fixed and growth mindset in a simple survey format and asks readers whether they agree or disagree with the statements:

1. Your intelligence is something very basic about you that you can't change very much.
2. You can learn new things, but you can't change how intelligent you are.
3. No matter how much intelligence you have, you can always change it quite a bit.
4. You can always substantially change how intelligent you are.

Statements one and two reflect the fixed mindset, and statements three and four represent the growth mindset. Dweck goes on to describe that the fixed and growth mindset can be applied to changing your personality, your career and other aspects of your life and ambition.

Developing a growth mindset is crucial for personal and professional development in school, business, sports, management and personal relationships. People who have a fixed mindset believe that you are a certain kind of person and nothing can change that. The fixed mindset person believes that you can do certain things differently, but important things about you can't be changed. The growth mindset person, however, believes that you can change who you are no matter what kind of person you are. The growth mindset person can always grow into the person he or she wants to become. Here I will present examples of how using the growth mindset inspired great achievements and personal accomplishments. As long as we are willing to put in the extra time, effort and determination required to improve our skills set, anything is possible.

The Growth Mindset in Action

Jaime Escalante

Jaime Escalante believed that math was the gateway to achievement in life and promoted this growth mindset among his students at Garfield High School in East Los Angeles. When Escalante started teaching at Garfield, East Los Angeles was known for its low-income households, drugs, and gangs. The school itself was in danger of losing its accreditation. Many thought Escalante's Mexican-American students were "unteachable." Escalante, however, believed in their abilities to do harder math than they were assigned as part of their curriculum. He encouraged his students to find the will, the desire and the motivation to learn enough to pass the Advanced Placement Calculus exam.

In 1982, 18 of Escalante's students took the Advanced Placement Calculus examination and passed. The group went on to lead successful careers in science, banking, and law.

Jim White

Another teacher who changed the mindset of his students was Jim White. Jim White started coaching cross country running at McFarland High School in 1980. McFarland is a farming town located in the central valley of California just outside Bakersfield. The school is a block away from the Central Valley Correctional Facility.

By 1987, White had coached up his runners to compete in the inaugural California state championship. Coach White dedicated his life and efforts to leading practices for his team after they had helped their parents pick fruits and vegetables in the fields.

He constantly helped the families with fundraisers to buy uniforms and travel to track competitions around the world. He led his teams to become state champions in 1987, 1992, 1993, 1994, 1995, 1996, 1999, 2000 and 2001. He retired from coaching teaching in 2003.

ASK FOR MORE

J.B. Bernstein

In 2007, J.B. Bernstein, a sports agent, went to India to create a new baseball sensation by looking for talent in a place that knew next to nothing about baseball. Bernstein believed that if Yao Ming could create a sensation on the basketball scene, Indian baseball players could also become a novelty.

In 2008, over 38,000 Indian hopefuls showed up for a chance to win $100,000 and a chance to train for the big leagues in the United States. Rinku Singh and Dinesh Patel were javelin throwers who had no previous experience with baseball before competing in the reality show, *Million Dollar Arm*, which was organized by J.B. Bernstein.

Rinku Singh pitched a ball at an unprecedented 89 miles per hour, and won first place, instantly becoming the richest man in his village outside Mumbai, India. Patel was the runner-up, with a pitching speed of 87 Miles per hour.

They followed Bernstein back to Los Angeles and trained for eight straight months under major league pitching coach at USC, Tom House. They performed for 20 major league scouts and were signed by the Pittsburgh Pirates. They went from their villages in India to become professional baseball players. They were to either become professional baseball players or return to their country to serve in the Indian army. With a growth mindset, anything is possible.

Growth Mindset Training

Now, Fortune 1000 companies are encouraging growth mindset training to encourage new and seasoned employees to change their outlook to increase their productivity and bottom line. Through surveys conducted, it was found that employees with a fixed mindset believed that only a small number of star employees are valued and respected while the work they performed didn't count. They were less committed to their work and didn't believe that the company had their best interests in mind. Growth mindset employees had a more positive outlook on their work for the company as a whole and felt that their work contributed a great deal to the overall improvements in the company's growth.

Action Steps

1. What is your mindset? Do you agree with Dr. Dweck's fixed and growth mindset statements?
2. Describe an experience where having a growth mindset helped you in your career or relationships.
3. Take the Mindset test:
   https://mindsetonline.com/testyourmindset/step1.php

24 Deep Practice

Even with a growth mindset, practice is essential to improve at any skill and make progress towards achieving mastery. Many people believe that expert performers are endowed with special talents or gifts acquired at birth and cultivated at a very young age. People believe that with these gifts, practice is almost unnecessary. No one is born an expert; he or she becomes skilled through practice and perseverance. The only genetic difference that counts at birth is height for basketball or horse jockeying.

Anders Ericsson, author of the paper *The Role of Deliberate Practice in the Acquisition of Expert Performance* and co-author of *Peak: Secrets of the New Science of Expertise*, states that only through deliberate practice can we achieve the heights of mastery and achievement. The author believes that we all have a "gift" to success and that gift is the inherent adaptability to overcome and learn from mistakes that we make and make decisions to change and grow through them. Ericsson believes that to achieve true mastery at any skill or sport one has to achieve at least 10,000 hours of deliberate practice. This idea was highlighted in the book *Outliers*, by Malcolm Gladwell. Anders Ericsson's studied violin players who started practicing at age five and continued throughout their childhoods. Over time, expert players had engaged in 10,000 hours of deliberate practice and could be considered masters. So, seven years of deliberate practice is required to achieve mastery in any field.

The author describes different types of practice. There are three types of practice. Naïve practice is just doing the same thing over and over again. The author uses driving as an example for naïve practice, since most adults repeat the process over and over again and do it by rote, without making any improvements. On the contrary, when we perform an activity, again and again, we might get sloppy and even get worse at doing it. Purposeful and deliberate practice, on the other hand, is practice with a goal tied to it. Top performers break down a skill into distinct parts and then focus on the aspect of the skill that needs improvement. They carry out the skill in the presence of a teacher or a coach so that the skill can be improved through repeated practice.

In his book *Talent is Overrated*, Geoff Colvin, editor of Fortune Magazine, breaks down deliberate practice into five different elements:

1. Practice is designed to improve performance. Deliberate practice must be goal oriented with clear objectives and goals specific to improving skills that are required in the skills that are being practiced.
2. The practice must be repeated consistently. Michael Phelps had 6-hour workouts six days a week, despite holidays and even his birthday. Ted Williams hit baseballs until his hands bled. Michael Jordan is famous for saying: "I've missed over 9000 shots in my career. I've lost almost 300 games. Over 26 times I have been trusted to take the game-winning shot and missed."
3. Feedback must be available during practice. Colvin believes that one can't progress without proper feedback. Without feedback, you might not be motivated to continue practicing. Coaches and teachers are great at giving objective feedback since with certain skills; it's sometimes hard to gauge if you are alone.

4. Deliberate practice is very demanding mentally. It is an effort of intense focus and concentration. Deliberate practice means that you are constantly correcting mistakes that you are making. Also through using mental representation, you can improve on skills that have already been perfected.
5. Deliberate practice is uncomfortable. By identifying our mistakes and our faults, we repeat them to improve on them.

One example of intense, deliberate practice is the training schedule of U.S. figure skating national champion Jeremy Abbot. In one typical training session, Jeremy usually skates 45-60 minutes. He has several coaches, a primary coach, technique coaches for jumps and spins, and choreographers who help him with dance routines. He does speed work, aerobic skating, 5-10 repetitions of the 7 or so triple jumps in his routine for a total of up to 50 jumps at a force of 7 times the weight of his body on each landing. He also includes a quadruple jump 5-10 times, which adds up to 125-175 jumps daily. He often runs programs back to back or blends them together by incorporating jumps and dance moves in varying intervals. Talk about deep practice!

Every time we practice a skill, a new layer of myelin is added to our neurons allowing us to retain new knowledge and skills. Deep practice is crucial to our development. Every time we practice a skill, circuits in our brain which controls our thoughts and movements are illuminated.

ASK FOR MORE

Every thought is created by chains of nerve fibers carrying small impulses like signals traveling through a circuit. Every time something is practiced these nerve fibers are coated in myelin, which acts as a layer of insulation around the nerve fiber. The thicker the myelin gets, the better it coats our nerve fibers, and the faster our movements and thoughts become. As we engage in deeper practice, the thicker the myelin gets and the faster our thoughts and movements get. All skills rely on the growth of myelin. It is created most quickly during childhood but continues to develop throughout life. Every skill, from bowling to tennis can be improved by practicing it repeatedly. Practice helps us to improve by sharpening our neural circuitry. We create myelin most effectively when we engage in the deep or deliberate practice.

In *The Talent Code*, Daniel Coyle describes the creation of myelin as rubber that surrounds copper wire. Whether you are swinging a baseball bat or learning how to play guitar, it all comes down to building myelin. Through deep practice or deliberate practice, one gets out of the comfort zone and stretch yourself beyond the skills which you have already learned. The struggle is a biological requirement for building myelin. Just like you can build muscles through strength training, you can build myelin through mental growth. Michelangelo, Coyle writes became a stone master when he was six years old and learned how to cut stone before he could write. Greatness grows through deliberate practice. Coyle insists that the only way to develop mastery in yourself is by igniting your passion and taking massive action consistently. Mastery of any skill is achievable.

Deep practice in any field can only be achieved through getting reliable feedback about our mistakes and weaknesses. If employees at our organizations today are not told how to develop their skills they won't grow. They will continue to perform at the level they are capable of for several years until they plateau or become obsolete. Many leaders of large companies such as CEO's have received coaching and mentoring to become who they are today. Jeff Fettig, CEO of Whirlpool said: "I am here today in part due to a handful of people, who before it was in vogue, provided coaching and mentoring early in my career. That helped me to develop."

In the next chapter, I will show the importance of teachers, coaches, and mentors in offering us the guidance and feedback we need to accomplish our goals and achievements. Many of the best coaches and teachers were experts themselves before they started to coach or teach others the skills which they have mastered. Often, becoming better means getting a better teacher or coach until mastery is achieved.

Action Steps

1. Choose a skill that you want to master. Break that skill into five sub-skills.
2. Hire a coach to help you achieve mastery. What are ten qualifications that you are looking for in a coach?

Coaching

From the start, Coach Ken Carter's practices were unorthodox. When he came on board to coach freshmen, junior varsity, and varsity basketball at Richmond High School in Northern California, he implemented strict rules for all to follow who played for him. When he first opened the season with his new players, he had them sign contracts which stipulated that academic performance off the court would weigh heavily towards their opportunity to play on the team. Carter would check grades every two weeks, and his players' teachers cooperated with him so that he and the staff were also on the same page. If a player fell short, he would postpone a game and even once threatened to forfeit a league's opening game. His tactics made the headlines around the United States in January of 1999, when despite his team's 13-0 record, Coach Ken Carter locked out his players. There would be no practices and no games until the players' grades improved because many of the players had broken the 19-point pledge they signed at the beginning of the season which stated they had to get good grades and perfect attendance in their classes. They also promised to study 10 hours a week and to always sit in front of the class.

Ken Carter believed that by putting education before basketball, he was teaching his players to become productive citizens responsible for themselves, on and off the court. Carter felt that even though he had coached his athletes to be the best in their division, their efforts and talents on the court weren't enough. Athletes must obey the rules and succeed in the classroom first.

During the first week of the lockout, there was no access allowed. During the second week, the team played two previously scheduled games, but they were not allowed to practice. The team won both games and moved on to the state tournament, but didn't make it to the finals that season.

His methods worked, as unusual as they were. During Carter's tenure (1997–2002) every one of his players graduated from Richmond High School. All received athletic or academic scholarships because of the discipline and restraint that Coach Carter taught them.

> *"The kids I was dealing with were inner-city kids, and most of them coming from single-parent homes. We exposed them to the real world of business, taking them on trips to Silicon Valley. We encouraged them to think big and dream big."*
>
> Coach Ken Carter

John Wooden is another example of a coach who believed that a good education was crucial to the success of his players. Raised on a farm in Southern Indiana, John Wooden was brought up on very basic principles that he emulated and taught to his players. His father had taught him three basic ideas that he passed on to his players. "Don't whine; don't complain and don't make excuses—just do your best."

He taught his players to put forth their best effort and believed that the positive results would show up because of their best efforts. He also taught his players what his father had taught him and his brothers. He told them that they should never try to be better than someone else and always learn from others.

John Wooden believed that success is defined by attaining the self-satisfaction of knowing that you made the best effort you're capable of making. If you are trying to improve the situation that currently exists for you that in and of itself is a success. Wooden's personal philosophy was not defined by wins or losses but in the daily development of oneself. Nonetheless, he was a winner as a coach and a legend in the personal growth industry. He served for 40 years as a head basketball coach. He led his teams to 12 Final Four appearances and won 10 National Championships during his career.

He established the *Pyramid of Success*, a blueprint that he wrote based on principles that he lived by such as best effort and hard work. His sphere of influence in athletic circles and leadership remains relevant and far-reaching today. Bill Walton, who played under John Wooden for four years at UCLA, said that Wooden never even talked about basketball, but used it as a vehicle to talk about life and inspire his players.

Like John Wooden, eminent pitching coach Tom House played the game he coached first. Tom House was a professional pitcher in the major leagues between 1971 and 1978. During his career, he pitched for the Atlanta Braves; the Boston Red Sox and the Seattle Mariners before retiring to become a pitching coach for various teams. During his pitching career, he earned a 3.79 ERA and had played in 536 major league innings.

ASK FOR MORE

As a pitching coach, Tom House worked with pitching and football legends Nolan Ryan, Drew Brees, and Tom Brady, and others. House worked with his staff for twenty years to analyze the throwing motions of quarterbacks and how force and technique applied to pitching baseball. Based on House's experience with pitchers, football quarterbacks sought his help. House said. "to get the best information we have to move them better physically, mechanically, nutritionally and emotionally." House and his staff attached sophisticated sensors to football players' bodies, and they used the information to get a three-dimensional readout of the range of motion to analyze the player's performance and suggest improvements.

What the coaches I have presented here all have in common are philosophies and techniques to bring out the best performance and character in their players. All had played the game which they coached and, of course, knew a great deal about technique and how to refine it through practice. The technique was important but often incidental to the other values that the coaches lived by such as hard work, discipline and putting forth one's best effort all the time. Coaches provide objective feedback, insight, and guidance to players and individuals so that they could improve their lives on and off the field.

Ken Carter had his contract, John Wooden had his pyramid, and Tom House had his technology. All three brought out the very best in the players they coached. They didn't focus solely on technique. They mainly taught the players to believe in themselves and understand that the game is the victory lap. The real work takes place during practices and scrimmages. The physical and mental preparation is what counts. If players put forth their best effort, they will be successful in the game and life.

Good coaches encourage failure and perseverance in their players. It's crucial that coaches review mistakes with their players and offer feedback about technique and mindset so that they improve their game and themselves. Coaches acknowledge individual's progress and recognize their strengths and weaknesses. Coaches convince their players about the power of hard work and putting forth the best effort. Coaches teach the power of teamwork and uniting together for a common goal.

ASK FOR MORE

Action Steps

1. Take the John Wooden training. Go to https://www.thewoodeneffect.com/ to enroll in Coach Wooden's *Framework of Success*.
2. Why is academic success so important for success on the field? Explain.
3. What is more important: technique or attitude? Explain.

Ask For Success

26 The Meaning of Success

Sometimes we find the meaning of success in unexpected places. In the movie *The Family Man* (2000, Directed by Brett Ratner), we meet Jack Campbell (Nicolas Cage), a single Wall Street Master of the Universe ready to close a billion dollar pharmaceutical merger on Christmas Eve. After a random act of kindness in a liquor store where Jack averts an act of violence by purchasing a $200 lottery ticket from Cash (Don Cheadle), he wakes up on Christmas Day in his suburban New Jersey home with his wife, Kate (Tea Leoni) and their children. Clearly, Jack is bewildered and confused, so he drives the family minivan back to New York City to return to his penthouse apartment and his office tower job as an investment banker. Cash tells him that what he is experiencing is a glimpse into the life he could have led had he not left to study finance in London and become a broker. He works as a manager at his father-in-law's retail tire store, owns a four-bedroom house in the suburbs and shares childcare duties with his wife, Kate, a non-profit lawyer. Jack grows accustomed to his new life as a family man until he meets the chairman of his former investment firm who offers Jack a chance at working as a broker at the firm. When Jack tells Kate about the new job, she implores him to be grateful for the life which they already have.

The epiphany of appreciating his new family life is short lived when upon seeing Cash again—this time as a store clerk, Jack asks to keep his life the way it is. When he wakes up, he is once again transported back to his former life as a wealthy investment banker on the verge of closing a big merger deal. He desperately tries to find Kate, who is preparing to leave New York City to open an office in Paris. Like Jack, she never married but focused her energies on her career as a lawyer.

Success is a choice. We make decisions all the time, and the decisions we make have power. In the movie, Jack became an investment banker and went to London to study finance and apply his skills at an investment firm in New York, where he was highly successful and driven.

ASK FOR MORE

Kate was a very successful lawyer who ran a very lucrative practice in New York City but wanted to expand to Europe.

In Jack's alternate universe, they are both successful as parents and at building a family. Jack is a loving father who learns of his new responsibilities such as changing diapers, dropping the youngest off at daycare before work and walking the dog. Arnie (Jeremy Piven), Jack's next door neighbor and bowling partner, reminds Jack that he has four bedrooms and a beautiful family that he shouldn't take it for granted. Arnie tells Jack that being a family man is a choice.

The movie resonates with many people because it proves to the viewer the realization that in life, or in any quest for personal growth, there is no single formula for personal success. Since we all have different goals, priorities, and standards, we can't all achieve the same level of success that will satisfy each of us. When you are truly successful, you understand what is important to you as an individual, and you look to achieve value and meaning in your life. Success is when you have achieved an objective or accomplished a certain goal that you had set for yourself. Success can also be described as a social status that describes a person who has achieved a level of material wealth and fame because of a favorable outcome of one's goal or objective.

RICHARD BELLMAN

The term *success* usually implies material wealth in return for one's work or services; however, your definition may be completely different from someone else's definition. As you continue on your journey, it is important that you define success for yourself. By being aware of what accomplishing a goal and achieving success means to you, attaining it will be easier. While many people consider owning a mansion and luxury cars and other luxuries as achieving success, many people feel that true happiness, health, and family ties are symbols of success in life.

Zig Ziglar believed that if you help enough people get what they want, you will get what you want. In other words, the true meaning of success and personal satisfaction goes way beyond money and material wealth. Your success will depend on the level of contribution that you plan on making to the world. If people could live a better life because of your contribution, your book, screenplay, idea or patent, then you are a success. If what you did was acting in the service of others and you created something that benefitted society then you are a success.

There are some people in the world who achieved success in terms of wealth accumulated for a book, project, or movie or publicly traded business, but this success doesn't equal happiness. A person doesn't need material wealth to be happy. Happiness is a feeling, a state of being whereas success is something to be attained or accomplished. Success can be measured in terms of wealth or material success, whereas happiness is infinite. Happiness could come from personal achievement or raising a family, whereas success is always considered to be a measure of one's personal worth or potential.

All around us, we see athletes who earn outlandish salaries for playing sports, and celebrities who earn several million dollars for their acting work in movies. Success and material wealth don't equate with happiness. Many wealthy people are lonely and depressed. Michael Jackson, Robin Williams, Phillip Seymour Hoffman and Prince are but a few celebrities who died wealthy and successful but very isolated from the society that they served with their talents. Many successful people often run through their money quickly and often have to rebuild or find new jobs or careers because of their poor money-management skills. In 12 seasons of playing in the NBA, Antoine Walker earned over $110 Million between 1996 and 2008. But, by 2010, two years after retiring from basketball, he was forced to file bankruptcy. Walker earned what 110 men could only hope to earn in a lifetime making $50,000 a year and had nothing to show for it.

Also, many people think that to achieve success we must make sacrifices. Many successful people have no children because they chose not to. All success is a personal choice. Success is the final culmination of all decisions that we make in our lives. I don't believe that one has to sacrifice having children to become successful in life, I don't believe that we have to sacrifice our health to become successful. I don't believe that we have to sacrifice our well-being and happiness in exchange for personal success.

Personal success is all about your perspective. If you value your family life and your marriage and have managed to stay together for many years with a man or woman whom you love and trust, then you are a successful spouse. If you were capable of raising a child from birth to adulthood, then you are a successful parent. If you have a job that you enjoy doing and feel that it provides a vital product or service to the world, then you have a successful career. If you can preserve your health throughout your life and maintain stable social relationships, then people will know you as a successful and happy person. If you can live your life happily, on your terms, then you are a successful person.

Do what makes your heart sing! Be proud of all of your accomplishments and try to make a significant contribution to society. Your success can bring happiness to others. If personal success means enough to you that you will sacrifice your time, energy and devotion to it, then show your talent to the world. If your contribution is so outstanding that nothing will get in your way so that you

ASK FOR MORE

accomplish all of your dreams, then success will surely follow your determination. Success is a culmination of all of your efforts, a positive outcome for all of the hard work and effort that you put into your accomplishments. Once you achieve success, you will have to work even harder to hold on to it. As you climb the ladder of success, your level of influence increases and your level of contribution to the world increases. As you ask for more success, the world will ask for more of you.

Action Steps

1. What does success mean for you? Write down five reasons that motivate you to achieve success.
2. If you could do one thing at which you would be guaranteed personal success, what would it be? Why haven't you started yet?

27   Why We Fail

While we all want success, why do so few of us achieve it? Here, I will take a look at some of the reasons why we fail at achieving success.

Just as there are many ways to define success, there are many ways to fail. Most prominent among personal growth experts is having a life's purpose. Most people are fortunate if they know their life's purpose early on in life. If you know as a child that you want to be the best athlete in your field, then starting early to work on your skills will give you a definite edge.

"Tiger" Eldrick Woods, for example, was said to have been born with an exceptional talent for golf. It helped that Earl and Kultida Woods gave their only son a putter as a toddler and entered him into various tournaments. By the time he was eight, after several lessons from his father, he was quite proficient in the game. By the age of 21, Tiger Woods was the youngest man to win the U.S. Masters at Augusta in 1997. He was also the first African-American.

Harlan Sanders didn't know his life purpose until later in his life. In fact, his life was a series of failures and personal defeats and disappointments. His father died when Harlan was five. He dropped out of school at age 16. By age 17 he had burned through four different jobs. He worked as a railroad conductor for four years between the ages of 18 and 22. He became a father at age 19, and at age 20, his wife left him and took their daughter. He was a failure as a soldier in the army, was rejected from law school, and failed as an insurance salesman. He finally landed a job as a dishwasher and cook in a small café. He retired at age 65 and later received his first pension check worth $105. He felt like a failure and thought about his life's purpose and all of the things he hadn't done with his life. But he knew how to cook. He used $87.00 of the pension money to buy ingredients to fry chicken and sold the finished product to his neighbors door to door. By age 88, he had built a fried chicken empire.

ASK FOR MORE

Having a great life purpose should inspire you to succeed. By having a clear life's purpose, you are more motivated to take action towards realizing that purpose for yourself and others. Even when you feel uninspired, or there are obstacles in your way, by having a clear life purpose you power through your problems or you find a way to overcome them. By living your life with purpose, you move out of your comfort zone to achieve your goals and bring them to fruition. Having a clear life purpose will not only give your life greater meaning, but you will achieve greater focus since it will prevent you from changing jobs and relationships as often. A life lived with purpose can give you greater meaning and hope for the future. Without having a clear purpose in your life, success is more difficult.

We fail because we don't believe that success is possible for us. We might feel that we don't have what it takes to achieve it. As Alfred Bandura pointed out in his theory of self-efficacy, if you think you can achieve success, then you will. If you believe that you can't, then you won't.

Optimistic thinking will always lead to steady and persistent action which in turn will produce better results. Martin Seligman believes that optimism is learned. Pessimists most always hit their goal on a series of tests every time because that is what they believed they would accomplish. Optimists most often exaggerated the results on tests and missed their targeted outcomes and believed they should try different approaches to achieving better outcomes. Also, as we will see later in the next chapter about attracting success to your life if your subconscious mind believes that something is possible for you, it will inform your level of effort and expectations of your body and behavior. You must believe in your ability to succeed.

We fail in life because we feel that we aren't worthy of success as if success is a gift, something we get for being a good person. Success is not based on merit. Success can be achieved through perseverance, hard work, and dedication to one's dream. We may have buried beliefs of low self-esteem and feelings of undeservedness. We have been told by so many people, friends, and unfortunately especially family that we will never amount to anything so we might as well give up on our dreams. We stop ourselves and fulfill others opinions and beliefs of us. We conform, and we give in and continue living a life of mediocrity.

You may feel like an imposter as you achieve success. Coined by psychologists Pauline Clance and Suzanne Imes, *The Imposter Syndrome* is when successful people, despite their obvious success, feel they are frauds and dismiss their success as being the result of luck or timing. They don't take credit for their success or internalize their success as being the actual result of their efforts and determination.

ASK FOR MORE

Lack of determination and persistence may be the reason for failure. Many people give up too easily in the face of adversity, loss, resistance and setbacks. Many people who admire the successful set—the celebrities, actors and rock stars—feel that they will never measure up to their status. We don't fully commit to our dreams or make any long-term goals because we might be setting ourselves up for failure. There are no overnight successes; anyone who has ever been successful will tell you that success came with a side of struggle and perseverance for dessert. Success requires patience. Everything happens at the right time.

We fail because we are too distracted. In a recent USA Today snapshot it said that Americans on average look at screens 7 hours a day. Many people check their cell phones up to 85 times a day, which accounts for around 4-6 hours, browsing the web, using email and apps. Social media apps such as Instagram, Twitter, YouTube, Facebook, and Snapchat occupy two hours of people's time on average. According to author Thomas Corley in his book *Rich Habits: The Daily Success Habits of Wealthy Individuals*, 67% of rich people watch TV for one hour or less per day. A total of 88% of the wealthy preferred to read for their personal growth. Successful people work longer hours, meditate every day, focus on their goals, write to-do lists the night before and manage their money. Success requires focus and determination; the distraction will lead to failure if you don't devote enough time to your goals.

The first sign of failure is casting blame on others. We fail because we don't take responsibility for ourselves. We make excuses for everything instead of taking responsibility for what happens in our lives. When life happens to us, we have to take responsibility for what happens in our lives and work to turn things around. Once we start to blame other for our failures, it is clear that we have not only failed, but we feel like failures.

Lastly, we fail because we don't want to be different. We don't want to stand out from the crowd. People don't like it when other people they know change or do something that makes them feel insecure about themselves. By pushing ourselves to succeed, we might remind people we know of their failures or dreams that weren't realized. When you attempt to excel at something that others haven't tried or felt they couldn't do, people feel intimidated and insecure. When you want to do something that you have never done before, something incredible, then you have to become comfortable with being different. Either people will be jealous of you, or they will support you. Many will resent you at first because you are showing them that you want to be different from them. Get used to being different because you are! Become confident with your dreams and desires, and they will lead you to your success.

Action Steps

1. How much time do you spend on social media?
2. What is the last non-fiction book you read?
3. Take the Success Likelihood test:
   https://www.psychologytoday.com/test/1332

28 Attract Success Into Your Life

You are where you are in life because of a series of choices you made. We make choices based on rational thoughts. Whatever the mind can conceive, the mind can believe and achieve. We are what we think about all day; this means we attract into our lives whatever we direct our conscious attention. We can take our minds and direct it towards what we want most in life. When you speak lack thoughts, poverty, joblessness, complaining, we will manifest more negativity. When we think positive we can direct our conscious minds towards the things we want.

RICHARD BELLMAN

The law of attraction states that your thoughts are creating your reality. What you focus on expands. If you experience negative thoughts and feelings, you attract negative events into your life. When you think positive thoughts, you will attract positive events into your life. You will send out positive energy into the world when you focus on what you want in life. Your thoughts about what you want most in life will create positive emotions about those things, and you will take massive action towards realizing your goal. Many people don't attract what they want in life because their conscious mind tells them that what they most truly want isn't possible for them. When people think of what they want, they shut it down because they get caught up in the "how" of achieving it.

Our thoughts shape our future reality. Once you create positive affirmations of what you want, you can imprint these thoughts into your subconscious to shape your reality. What we believe determines what we make true. How we think of ourselves is determined by our beliefs. Alter a reality, and we can alter our beliefs. When we start to visualize success, these images fuel our beliefs which strengthen our potential to take massive action towards achievement which then strengthens our beliefs.

Since the mind cannot tell the difference between real or imagined thoughts, it will relay to the subconscious whatever it receives; this is the power of visualization.

ASK FOR MORE

Once you have a clear image of your goal, imagine it coming into reality in your mind. If you can see it in your mind's eye, you can hold it in your hand. Since the law of attraction is a function of your intention, it will work in your favor if you believe it will. Ask, believe and then receive. In other words, this is the basic tenet of the law of attraction. Many people "try" the law of attraction, but when they see it doesn't work for them, they give up. They don't get instant gratification from their efforts, so they stop asking the universe for what they want. They stop believing that it will manifest for them, and they stop receiving the benefits of the law of attraction.

For the law of attraction to work in your favor, you must believe first and see later. Many people follow the scientific method: seeing is believing. The law of attraction makes us put faith first; then believe, and then see. Taking action and taking advantage of opportunities that come your way is crucial to the manifestation of your dreams.

Let's say that you are looking for work or a better paying job. If you remain positive and network with as many people as you can, the law of attraction will help you. If you set goals for yourself such as sending at least five job applications and resumes every day for six weeks, you will start seeing results. If you show up on time and well-dressed to every interview you are called for, you will see positive results. You will be favored by the law of attraction for your efforts and positive outlook. New opportunities will come your way if you maintain a positive outlook.

Many athletes, musicians, and performers rely on the power of visualization to improve themselves constantly and move their art towards the levels of mastery.

One of the most advanced forms of visualization is known as mental chess. Experienced chess players are experienced at playing the game without a board or pieces. Players imagine the board, play and then keep track of the positions taken during the game.

Activist Anatoly Sharansky, who fought for Soviet human rights, used the game of mental chess to survive his prison sentence. In 1977, he was falsely accused of spying for the United States. He was sentenced to spend nine years in prison, which included 400 days in solitary confinement in a freezing 5 foot by 6-foot cell. It was during this period of intense sensory deprivation that would normally break other prisoners down that Sharansky developed his skills of mental chess. He played both sides, white and black for months on end, holding the whole game in his head. With the help of Western pressure and agencies who fought for his release, Anatoly Sharansky became an Israeli cabinet minister. When world chess champion Garry Kasparov played against the cabinet, he was able to beat everyone but Sharansky at the game.

Visualization works very well in sports practice as well. A study recently conducted at the University of Chicago by Dr. Biasiotto proved this point. He split people into three groups. The first group was asked to practice shooting free throws every day for an hour. The second group was asked to simply visualize the ball falling through the net every day for an hour. This group intensely visualized success by feeling the ball roll off their fingers. They saw the ball travel through the air, with a perfect arc and watched their hands bend as they followed through with the shot. Then they saw and heard the ball swish through the net. The third group was asked to do nothing.

The groups practiced their tasks for 30 days. After the 30 days, Dr. Biasiotto found the following results: The first group, which practiced using basketballs, improved their free throws by 24%. The second group, who only visualized their free throws, improved by an impressive 23% without ever touching a basketball. The third group didn't improve, which was, of course, expected because they didn't do anything. Visualization has great power towards attracting success into our lives.

Visualizing is seeing that you already have that what you want. You use your imagination to conjure what you want and even feel grateful for having it when you don't have it yet. Daily visualization exercises will speed your achievement of all of your goals and whatever it is you want in life. Though visualization you tell the universe what it is that you want and set the forces in motion to attain it.

Many of us have a hard time with visualization because we are only capable of seeing what is in front of us or what surrounds us. If you are living in a small bachelor apartment, you might think it is absurd to visualize yourself living in a mansion or at the very least a house of your own. However, by using your imagination, you are pushing away any attitude of lack that you might have by thinking it isn't possible by dwelling on the idea as being real now. You already have it.

You can choose to change anything you want about yourself and in your life. You have the power to visualize life as you want it to be. If you want to heal your body, lose weight, or find your soulmate you have the power to visualize your ultimate goal and manifest your desires in your life.

Arnold Schwarzenegger, five-time Mr. Universe, and four-time Mr. Olympia believed that as long as the mind can envision the fact that you can do something, you can. If you believe that you have already achieved a certain goal that you want, then it is yours for the taking. It's mind over matter. In a 1976 newspaper interview while he was promoting his movie, *Stay Hungry*, Arnold proclaimed that he was going to be the number one Hollywood Box-Office movie star. He had an Austrian accent, a huge body, and wasn't exactly star material. Nonetheless, he said the process is the same for bodybuilding and becoming a movie star. The key to the law of attraction is to create a vision of who you want to be and step into that picture as if it were already true. True to form, Schwarzenegger took massive action towards acting as he had done towards body building. He took acting classes, speech classes, and voice classes to reduce his accent. He has an outstanding 61 credits in major feature films, and many of those are starring roles.

Action Steps

1. What is one thing about yourself that you would like to change? How can the law of attraction help you in achieving your goal?
2. Take your main goal, and create five goals underneath it, and then another five goals to achieve your meta-goals. Create a goal tree and grow it for 30 days.

Regrets: What Gets Left Behind

Living a successful life means being able to live a life that is unique and aligned with your values and beliefs. If today was your last day, would it make a difference if you stayed an extra two hours after work? Perhaps those two hours could have been spent with people you care about like children or friends who want your attention. Living a successful life is one without many regrets. When you are going to die, material wealth and the trappings of success like houses, cars, jewelry don't count. People who are at the end of their journey in life are astounded at how fast their life went and can't believe that it is coming to an end. Your true mission and ideals come to the surface when you know that the end is near or at least, fast approaching. Your success in life is a matter of perspective, personal fulfillment, and creative meaning.

Bronnie Ware, an Australian singer, and songwriter, was looking for a job that had personal meaning and a way to avoid paying rent or a mortgage. She found both as a palliative care worker, tending to patients who were about to die. In her book, *The Top Five Regrets of the Dying*, Ms. Ware indicates the top five regrets which most of her patients expressed to her during her eight-year career.

- The first regret was, "I wish I'd had the courage to live a life true to myself, not the life that others expected of me." Individuals who were near the end of their lives typically felt that they had lived their lives based on what other people expected of them. Many people looked back on their lives and realized that they hadn't honored even half of their dreams. They were forced to accept this realization at the end of their lives knowing that it was because of the choices which they made or didn't make.

So often we are shaped by what other people are telling us what they think. We often are influenced by what we believe other people will think of us, and we worry about how others will perceive us. We often keep our ideas and our dreams hidden inside because we are afraid to be rejected by others or incur a loss of love or disapproval of us on their part.

The key take away from this first regret is that what other people think of you is none of your business. Seeking others' approval is a never ending battle. You will never be able to please anyone but yourself. The bottom line is that it's not if others approve of you but whether you approve of yourself. No matter what your age or circumstance live your life on your terms, not on someone else's.

- The second regret was, "I wish I didn't work so hard." Many of the patients who expressed this regret were men from certain generations. They missed out on spending time with their children and with their spouses or partners.

RICHARD BELLMAN

Many of us get so consumed by our jobs, careers and climbing the proverbial corporate ladder. We often even forget to leave work at work and either physically bring work home with us to complete in isolation, away from our family or even out of town hundreds of miles away from those we love. Sometimes we leave the physical workplace to be with our families, but with emails, texting, and constant connectivity to our jobs at all times; we aren't present for the people in our lives who count the most.

By striving to achieve a work-life balance and making conscious choices to turn our work button completely off, we can replenish our energy and focus so that we improve as human beings, and can become happier, and more productive people. By creating more space in our lives, we can find more creative meaning and engagement in activities away from work.

- The third regret is, "I wish I had the courage to express my feelings." Many people in Ms. Ware's care told her that they suppressed their true feelings to keep peace with others. Because of this, they settle for a timid, mediocre existence and never really grew to the people they were capable of actually becoming.

Carrying bitterness and resentment inside your heart towards people who put you down or didn't hear you out or take the time to understand your feelings can tear you up inside and lead to illness.

We often feel stifled by other people's opinions of us, but we don't take a stand against them to prove ourselves. This suppression of emotions may be based on real fears of retaliation if there is an imbalance of power in the relationship. It's still always healthy to admit one's true emotions and be in harmony with yourself and others.

- The fourth regret was, "I wish I had stayed in touch with my friends." Many of the people Ms. Ware cared for didn't realize the true value of maintaining friendships and having friends until their last few weeks of life when it was too late to find the people who they once cared about. If they were able to track them down, the mission was sometimes futile since their friends had already passed on themselves.

We get so completely caught up in the business of our lives that we forget about the people we used to know, people who shaped us during high school, adolescence, and college periods. Many people deeply regret not staying in touch with friends and giving friendships the time and effort which they deserved.

Even now, in the age of technology, it may be considerably easier to stay in touch with friends, but having connections that are lasting and genuine is another matter altogether. Texting, e-mailing, chatting and connecting on social networks seems forced and artificial at times. There is nothing that can authenticate the warmth of the human touch and the soothing sound of a familiar voice on the phone.

The takeaway here is to create friendships during life and cultivate them as you live so that you will not have the same regrets. Friends are our connection to our past. We can reminisce about the way life was for us at the same point in each of our lives. We can laugh about our former selves and place hope in the future by keeping our friendships strong.

- The fifth regret, "I wish I had let myself be happier" was a very common regret among the dying patients whom Ms. Ware spoke to during her career.

  Many people don't realize that happiness is a choice. We get stuck in old patterns and habits. We expect other people to make us happy, or we hope for things to make us happy, or money to make us happy. We wait for happiness and fulfillment that never comes. We often fear change and can't bring ourselves to break away from old habits or relationships which were broken to pursue our happiness. We cling to old values, careers, and mindsets. Happiness seems elusive, but it is always within our grasp. We only have to reach for it every day.

Success in life depends on your perspective. The insights that I showed you here will hopefully allow you to correct certain aspects of your life so that you minimize the impact of those regrets later in life. Now is the time to amend these regrets before it's too late. Think of the five regrets that Ms. Ware described in her book and see how they apply to your life and begin to make some changes where you see fit. True success in life is not because of material wealth, status or fame; it depends on your attitude towards life and other people. Enjoy the journey of life and appreciate all of the blessings which life has to offer you.

ASK FOR MORE

Action Steps

1. Think of the top five regrets. Which one best applies to your current situation. What can you do right now to change the course of your actions?
2. Try to find a friend that you knew when you were younger. Call him or her and catch up. How was the call? Did you establish a connection and build a regular schedule to keep in touch?

30 Gratitude and Success

Throughout this book, I have given you insights, ideas, and strategies to achieve success and true fulfillment in your life. Expressing gratitude for everything that you have in life will allow you to create a happier and more successful life.

Gratitude is an expression of your sincere thanksgiving for all of the good that has come into your life throughout your life. To achieve true success in life, we must first appreciate all that we have to achieve the richness and abundance that life has to offer. Many people who live in lack feel that they have no reason to be grateful. For them, life is a constant struggle. They endure constant hardship and pain, often struggling to make ends meet. By expressing gratitude for small blessings and appreciating what we have so far, we can achieve even greater abundance and success. Like the law of attraction, what we focus on expands. If we focus on lack thoughts, we will get lack results. If we focus on abundance and are grateful for what we have, we will receive more of what we want in life.

Having an attitude of gratitude is critical to achieving success. To receive abundance in the future while working on "it" or your dream, it is important that you are happy with what you have today. Instead of complaining about what isn't happening in your business or your life, focus on what is happening in your favor. Instead of thinking of how far you still have to go to reach your goals and achieve the level of success that you want, focus on how far you have already come. By appreciating your talents and your hard work, you will be more appreciative and grateful for small successes as they come into your life.

When we are grateful, we expect good things to come into our life. When we express our gratitude for all of the good that we have in our lives, we become more aware of life's abundance and opportunities. By showing our gratitude, we are enjoying the fruits our success, and this allows us to find more success in other areas of our lives. When our goals don't work out as we had originally planned, grateful people can learn from their failure and continue to reach their goals as planned. People who lack gratitude, on the other hand, may not be happy with their success and may never achieve true satisfaction with any measure of success that they achieve.

Grateful people are optimistic about the way they see the world. Since they are grateful for what they already have achieved in life and focus on what they want to achieve in their lives, their outlook on life is a positive one. Optimistic people are more generous, happier and are less frequently depressed. Optimists feel that when there is a negative setback in their lives, they can do something to change the outcome for the better. Pessimists, on the other hand, often feel helpless in the face of diversity and feel that nothing can be done to make a difference in the situation.

Gratitude can increase our levels of optimism and allow us to expect better things and events in our lives. People who have a dispositional leaning towards gratitude tend to focus on and expect good things to happen in their lives. Grateful optimists tend to consistently raise their expectations for positive aspects of their lives and reap the benefits when they are met! Expressing gratitude can reduce stress and anxiety through counting blessings in our lives instead of focusing on complaints. By focusing on positive aspects of one's daily life instead of focusing on the all- consuming negative aspects, we can reduce stress and improve our overall well-being. Expressing gratitude can also help one sleep better at night. By writing in a gratitude journal for fifteen minutes every night before going to sleep, participants in a study at the University of California Davis worried less at bedtime and slept better afterward. Having an attitude of gratitude and being aware of good things in your life can allow you to feel more relaxed and more refreshed the next day.

Expressing gratitude for what we have and what we are given is a choice that we make, just as we choose to be happy.

> *"Gratitude enriches human life."* Professor Robert Emmons, University of California, Davis

Gratitude elevates, energizes, inspires and transforms. People are moved, opened and humbled through expressions of gratitude. Having an attitude of gratitude can lead to a more optimistic outlook on life, greater productivity, and increased attitude to persevere at our goals. Gratitude can lead us closer to success in every way.

Once you achieve real material success and can provide the type of lifestyle that you have always wanted for yourself and your family, express your gratitude for your success. Make important and necessary monetary contributions to causes that you believe in so others won't have to struggle or suffer as much.

We hear of the wealthy donating millions or billions to universities and celebrities endorsing charitable causes with their names and images. Remember that you can have an impact as well. By making small monetary contributions to charitable causes, we can make a lasting impact.

Through volunteering our time, we can make a lasting impact. By visiting with people who want to hear your message of hope, your path to success, you can have a lasting impact on your community. By performing random acts of kindness, you can express your gratitude for your success by paying it forward.

In my next book, *The Benefits of Gratitude*, I explore the psychosocial benefits of expressing gratitude for everything that you have, acknowledging that it comes from an outside source. I am grateful that you have accompanied me on this journey. I hope you continue to ask for more in your work life, your relationships, and your health and longevity. By asking for more in our lives, we are accepting full accountability for everything that happens throughout our lives. By asking for more, we could create more fulfilling, healthier and more productive lives for ourselves. Remember that there is only one life to live, so live well and dream big. Ask for more of yourself and receive more in your life!

Action Steps

1. For thirty days, keep a Gratitude Journal. Write down 3-5 things for which you are grateful every day, and why.
2. Go to http://richardbellmanspeaks.com/gratitude-checklist/ and take the gratitude challenge.
3. Practice one random act of kindness for one week and see what kind of difference you can make in people's lives.

References

ASK FOR RESPONSIBILITY

Chapter 2: Start Here: Taking the Initiative
- Isidore, C., & Luhby, T. (2015, July 9). *Turns out Americans Work Really Hard...But Some Want to Work Harder.* Retrieved from http://money.cnn.com/2015/07/09/news/economy/americans-work-bush

Chapter 3: Take a Risk
- Burchard, B. (2012). *The Charge: Activating the 10 Human Drives That Make You Feel Alive.* New York: Free Press.
- History.com Staff. (2009). *Columbus Reaches the New World.* [Web log post]. Retrieved from http://www.history.com/this-day-in-history/columbus-reaches-the-new-world
- John F. Kennedy Presidential Library and Museum. [Web log post]. Retrieved from https://www.jfklibrary.org/JFK/JFK-in-History/Space-Program.aspx

- Szalay, J. (2013, August 28). *Hernán Cortés: Conqueror of the Aztecs.* Retrieved from http://www.livescience.com/39238-hernan-cortes-conqueror-of-the-aztecs.html
- *Risk Taking—Take a Risk.* (n.d.) [Web log post]. Retrieved from http://www.motivation-for-dreamers.com/risk-taking.html
- *What is Risk?* (n.d.) [Web log post]. New York University. Retrieved from http://people.stern.nyu.edu/adamodar/pdfiles/valrisk/ch1.pdf

Chapter 5: What's Your Motivation?
- Boundless. "*Incentive Theory of Motivation and Intrinsic vs. Extrinsic Motivation.*" Boundless Psychology Boundless. (2016, September 20). [Web log post]. Retrieved from https://www.boundless.com/psychology/textbooks/boundless-psychology-textbook/motivation-12/theories-of-motivation-65/incentive-theory-of-motivation-and-intrinsic-vs-extrinsic-motivation-252-12787/
- George Mallory, (n.d.) *Wikipedia.* Retrieved from https://en.wikipedia.org/wiki/George_Mallory

- Yahoo Travel Staff. (2014) *Deadliest Sport Ever? Why People Risk Their Lives Mountain Climbing.* Retrieved from https://www.yahoo.com/style/deadliest-sport-ever-why-people-risk-their-lives-87909897077.html

ASK FOR INCREASE

Chapter 6: Engagement and Expectations
- *6 Ways to Build Employee Engagement and Relationships in Your Company: Zappos Insights.* (2013, September 30). Retrieved from https://www.zapposinsights.com/blog/item/6-ways-to-build-employee-engagement-and-relationships-in-your-company
- Adkins, A. *Employee Engagement Stagnant in 2015.* (2016, January 13). Retrieved from http://www.gallup.com/poll/188144/employee-engagement-stagnant-2015.aspx
- Miller, A. (2009, October 31). *The Hawthorne Effect, Or a Lesson in the Power of a Story*: The Organizational Scientist. [Web log post]. Retrieved from https://organizationalscientist.wordpress.com/2009/10/31/the-hawthorne-effect-or-a-lesson-in-the-power-of-a-story/

- Money, J. (2014, October 8). *Study: "Pygmalion Effect" Links Teacher Expectations to Student Success.* Retrieved from http://blogs.edweek.org/teachers/teaching_now/2014/10/pygmalion_effect_links_teacher_expectations_to_student_success.html
- Pygmalion Effect, *Wikipedia.* Retrieved from https://en.wikipedia.org/wiki/Pygmalion_effect
- Rosenthal, R., & Fode, K. (1963). The effect of experimenter bias on performance of the albino rat. *Behavioral Science, 8.* (pp. 183-189). Robert Rosenthal's Work on Expectancy Effects http://psych.wisc.edu/braun/281/Intelligence/LabellingEffects.htm
- Spiegel, A. (2012, September 17). *Teachers' Expectations Can Influence How Students Perform.* Retrieved from http://www.npr.org/sections/health-shots/2012/09/18/161159263/teachers-expectations-can-influence-how-students-perform

Chapter 7: I Think I Can: The Power of the Will

- McGonigal, K. (2013, December 31). *The Willpower Instinct: How Self-Control Works, Why It Matters, and What You Can Do To Get More of It.* New York, NY: Penguin Group.

- *Pencils of Promise-Founder's Story.* (n.d.) Retrieved from https://pencilsofpromise.org/about/founders-story/
- Pinker, S. (2011, September 4). *The Sugary Secret of Self Control.* [Web log post]. Retrieved from http://www.nytimes.com/2011/09/04/books/review/willpower-by-roy-f-baumeister-and-john-tierney-book-review.html
- Samuel Pierpont Langley. (n.d.) *Wikipedia.* Retrieved from https://en.wikipedia.org/wiki/Samuel_Pierpont_Langley
- Theodore Herzl. (n.d.) *Wikipedia.* Retrieved from https://en.wikipedia.org/wiki/Theodor_Herzl

Chapter 8: Willpower and Self-Discipline
- Callahan, M. (2015, January 18). *The Brutal Secrets Behind The Biggest Loser.* [Web log post]. New York Post http://nypost.com/2015/01/18/contestant-reveals-the-brutal-secrets-of-the-biggest-loser/
- McGonigal, K. (2013, December 31). *The Willpower Instinct: How Self-Control Works, Why It Matters, and What You Can Do To Get More of It.* New York, NY: Penguin Group.

- Rivas, A. (2016, June 6). *Why Weight Loss is So Hard: An Interview with the Guy Who Studied The Biggest Loser.* Retrieved from http://www.medicaldaily.com/biggest-loser-weight-loss-psychology-armando-gonzalez-388709

Chapter 9: Procrastination and Other Roadblocks That We Put in Our Own Way

- Bichell, R. *Average Age of First Time Moms Keeps Climbing in the U.S.* (2016, January 14). Retrieved from http://www.npr.org/sections/health-shots/2016/01/14/462816458/average-age-of-first-time-moms-keeps-climbing-in-the-u-s
- Ferarri. J. (2010). *Still Procrastinating? The No-Regrets Guide to Getting it Done.* Hoboken, NJ: John Wiley & Sons.
- Marano, H.E. (2003, August 23). *Procrastination: Ten Things to Know, Psychology Today.* Retrieved from https://www.psychologytoday.com/articles/200308/procrastination-ten-things-know
- Pychyl, T. (2010, January 20). *Overcoming Procrastination: Four Potential Problems During Goal Pursuit.* Retrieved from https://www.psychologytoday.com/blog/dont-

delay/201001/overcoming-procrastination-four-potential-problems-during-goal-pursuit
- *Stop Procrastinating - Why People Procrastinate.* (n.d.) http://www.free-management-ebooks.com/faqps/procrastination-03.htm

Chapter 10: Execution, Effort and Excellence
- Beyonce. (n.d.) *Wikipedia.* Retrieved from https://en.wikipedia.org/wiki/Beyonc%C3%A9
- Biography.com Editors. (2016, August 17). *Joy Mangano Biography.com.* [Web log post]. Retrieved from http://www.biography.com/people/joy-mangano-05202015
- Johnson, R. (2008, October 3*). The Cantankerous Man behind the Wipers.* [Web log post]. Retrieved from http://articles.latimes.com/2008/oct/03/entertainment/et-kearns3
- Keller, G., & Papasan, J. (2013). *The One Thing: Planning for a Big Year with the 1-3-5 Rule.* [Web log post]. https://www.the1thing.com/time-management/planning-for-a-big-year-with-the-1-3-5-rule/
- Sharkey, J. (2010, October 4). *Reinventing the Suitcase by Adding the Wheel.* [Web log post]. Retrieved from

http://www.nytimes.com/2010/10/05/business/05road.html
- Usain Bolt. (n.d.) *Wikipedia*. Retrieved from https://en.wikipedia.org/wiki/Usain_Bolt

ASK FOR CHARACTER

Chapter 11: Courage:
- Chasing the Frog.com Editors. (n.d.) *Vince Papale-Invincible (2006)*. [Web log post]. Retrieved from http://www.chasingthefrog.com/reelfaces/invincible.
- Jacques, R. (2013, September 25). *16 Wildly Successful People Who Overcame Huge Obstacles To Get There*, [Web log post]. Retrieved from http://www.huffingtonpost.com/2013/09/25/successful-people-obstacles_n_3964459.html
- Hamilton, L. (2015, July 210. *4 Famous People Who Were Told They Would Never Achieve Their Goals*. [Web log post]. Retrieved from http://blog.fitplanapp.com/4-famous-people-who-were-told-they-would-never-achieve-their-goals/

Chapter 12: Faith
- Buchanan, J. (2016, July 28). *Albert Bandura: Self-Efficacy for Agentic Positive Psychology*. [Web log post]. Retrieved from

https://positivepsychologyprogram.com/bandura-self-efficacy/

Chapter 13: Patience
- Adam36. (n.d.) *The Key to Success is Patience.* [Web log post]. Retrieved from http://www.funtrivia.com/playquiz/quiz36550329d7690.html
- John A. Roeblin. (n.d.) *Wikipedia.* Retrieved from https://en.wikipedia.org/wiki/John_A._Roebling

Chapter 14: Integrity
- Dior, C. (n.d.) *7 Signs You are Lying to Yourself and You don't Know It.* [Web log post]. Retrieved from http://www.lifehack.org/352062/7-signs-you-are-lying-yourself-and-you-dont-know
- Manson, M. (2013, October 30). *9 Subtle Lies We Tell Ourselves.* [Web log post]. Retrieved from https://markmanson.net/9-subtle-lies-we-all-tell-ourselves

Chapter 15: Resilience
- American Psychological Association Staff Writer (n.d.) *The Road to Resilience.* Retrieved from http://www.apa.org/helpcenter/road-resilience.aspx

- Burkeman, O. (2002, September 17). *Man of Steel.* [Web log post]. Retrieved from https://www.theguardian.com/education/2002/sep/17/science.highereducation
- Frankl, V. E. (1984). *Man's Search for Meaning*, New York, NY: Washington Square Press.
- Sauchuk, S. R. (2013, December 9). *Resilience and Nelson Mandela.* [Web log post]. Retrieved from http://leadership.vfmac.edu/resilience-and-nelson-mandela/
- Victor Frankl. (n.d.)-*Wikipedia.* Retrieved from https://en.wikipedia.org/wiki/Viktor_Frankl

ASK FOR HEALTH

Chapter 16: Weight
- Cister, G. (2004). *In Fat Land*, New York, NY: Houghton Mifflin.
- Fox, M. (2016, June 7). *America's Obesity Epidemic Hits a New High.* [Web log post]. Retrieved from http://www.nbcnews.com/health/health-news/america-s-obesity-epidemic-hits-new-high-n587251
- Hammond, R. A. & Levine, R. (2010, August 20). *The Economic Impact of Obesity in the United States.* [Web log post] Retrieved from

https://www.ncbi.nlm.nih.gov/pmc/articles/PMC3047996/
- Rauh, S. (n.d.) *Is Fat the New Normal?* [Web log post.] Retrieved from http://www.webmd.com/diet/obesity/features/is-fat-the-new-normal#1
- Sena, M. (n.d.) *Fast Food Industry Analysis 2017- Costs and Trends.* [Web log post]. Retrieved from https://www.franchisehelp.com/industry-reports/fast-food-industry-report/
- Wansink, B. (2006). *Mindless Eating.* New York, NY: Bantam Dell.

Chapter 17: Exercise
- Harvard Medical School Staff Writer. (2014, March 13). *Healthy Mind, Healthy Body: Benefits of Exercise.* [Web log post]. Retrieved from https://hms.harvard.edu/sites/default/files/assets/Sites/Longwood_Seminars/Exercise3.14.pdf
- Jaslow, R. (2013, May 3). *CDC: 80 Percent of American Adults Don't Get Recommended Exercise.* [Web log post]. Retrieved from http://www.cbsnews.com/news/cdc-80-percent-of-american-adults-dont-get-recommended-exercise/
- Oaklander, M. & Jones, H. (2016, September 1). *7 Surprising Rx for Exercise, How Physical Activity*

Fortifies the Brain and Body. Time Magazine, September 12-19, Volume 188, NO. 10-11.
- Rothfield, L. (2015, May 15). *7 Companies with Amazingly Unique Wellness Programs*, [Web log post]. Retrieved from http://mashable.com/2015/05/15/unique-corporate-wellness-programs/#_rE.SMDNUEq9

Chapter 18: Sleep

- Anthony, A. (2017, January 22). *Why the Secret to Productivity Isn't Longer Hours.* [Web log post]. Retrieved from https://www.theguardian.com/money/2017/jan/22/alex-soojung-kim-pang-interview-rest-why-you-get-more-done-when-you-work-less
- Ghosh, P. (2015, May 15). *Why Do We Sleep?* [Web log post]. Retrieved from http://www.bbc.com/news/science-environment-32606341
- Harvard Education Staff Writer. (2007, December 18). *Why Do We Sleep, Anyway?* Retrieved from http://healthysleep.med.harvard.edu/healthy/matters/benefits-of-sleep/why-do-we-sleep
- Harvard Medical School of Medicine Staff Writer. (n.d.) *Sleep Performance and Public Safety.* [Web log post]. Retrieved from

http://healthysleep.med.harvard.edu/healthy/matters/consequences/sleep-performance-and-public-safety
- Harvard Medical School of Medicine Staff Writer. (n.d.) *Sleep and Disk Risk.* [Web log post]. Retrieved from http://healthysleep.med.harvard.edu/healthy/matters/consequences/sleep-performance-and-public-safety
- Harvard Medical School of Medicine Staff Writer. (n.d.) *Sleep, Learning and Memory.* [Web log post]. Retrieved from http://healthysleep.med.harvard.edu/healthy/matters/consequences/sleep-performance-and-public-safety
- Henry, Z. (2015, September 4). *6 Companies Where It's Ok To Nap.* [Web log post]. Retrieved from http://www.inc.com/zoe-henry/google-uber-and-other-companies-where-you-can-nap-at-the-office.html
- Huffington Post Staff. (2013, December 3). *5 Other Disastrous Accidents Related to Sleep Deprivation.* [Web log post]. Retrieved from http://www.huffingtonpost.com/2013/12/03/sleep-deprivation-accidents-disasters_n_4380349.html
- *Sleeping at Work: Companies with Nap Rooms and Snooze Friendly Policies.* (n.d.) [Web log post]. Retrieved from https://sleep.org/articles/sleeping-work-companies-nap-rooms-snooze-friendly-policies/

- Smith, M., Robinson, L., & Segal, R. (n.d.) *How Much Sleep Do We Really Need?* [Web log post]. Retrieved from https://www.helpguide.org/articles/sleep/how-much-sleep-do-you-need.htm
- *The Guide to Sleeping in Airports.* (n.d.) [Web log post]. Retrieved from http://www.sleepinginairports.net/
- Walker, M. (2015, April 15). *BBC-Earth: Apes Reveal Secrets to Good Sleep.* [Web log post]. Retrieved from http://www.bbc.com/earth/story/20150415-apes-reveal-sleep-secrets

Chapter 19: Companionship and Health

- Cacioppo, J. T. (n.d.) *Loneliness: Human Nature and the Need for Social Connection.* [Web log post]. Retrieved from http://www.campaigntoendloneliness.org/
- Cacioppo, J. T. (2016, February 28). *Loneliness is Like an Iceberg.* [Web log post]. Retrieved from https://www.theguardian.com/science/2016/feb/28/loneliness-is-like-an-iceberg-john-cacioppo-social-neuroscience-interview
- Evans. J. L. (2017, July 13). *Ten Good Things about Having a Life Partner.* [Web log post]. Retrieved from

https://pairedlife.com/relationships/Long-Term-Companionship-Advantages-of-Having-a-Life-Partner
- Gupta, S. (2015, August 4). *Why You Should Treat Loneliness as a Chronic Illness.* [Web log post]. Retrieved from http://www.everydayhealth.com/news/loneliness-can-really-hurt-you/
- Mayo Clinic Staff. (2016, September 28).*Friendships: Enrich Your Life and Improve Your Health.*[Web log post]. Retrieved from http://www.mayoclinic.org/healthy-lifestyle/adult-health/in-depth/friendships/art-20044860
- Slater, D. (2012, November 7). *What Harvard's Grant Study Reveals about Happiness and Life.* [Web log post]. Retrieved from http://www.thedailybeast.com/articles/2012/11/07/what-harvard-s-grant-study-reveals-about-happiness-and-life.html
- Szalavitz, M. (2013, March 26). *Social Isolation, Not Just Feeling lonely, May Shorten Lives.* [Web log post]. Retrieved from http://healthland.time.com/2013/03/26/social-isolation-not-just-feeling-lonely-may-shorten-lives/
- Vaillant, G. E. (2013, August 11). *Triumphs of Experience. The 75 Year Study That Found The Secrets to a Fulfilling Life.* [Web log post]. Retrieved from

- http://www.huffingtonpost.com/2013/08/11/how-this-harvard-psycholo_n_3727229.html
- Waite, L. J., & Gallagher, M. (2000). *The Case for Marriage: Why Married People Are Happier, Healthier and Better Off Financially.* New York, NY: Doubleday.

Chapter 20: Mindful Meditation and Health
- Aubrey, A. (2008, August 21). *To Lower Blood Pressure, Open Up and Say Om.* [Web log post]. Retrieved from http://www.npr.org/2008/08/21/93796200/to-lower-blood-pressure-open-up-and-say-om
- Huff, E. A. (2013, June 16). *Your Body On Meditation.* {Web log post]. Retrieved from http://www.naturalnews.com/040794_meditation_disease_prevention_stress_reduction.html
- Kabat-Zinn, J. (1994). *Wherever You Go, There You Are.* New York, NY: Hyperion.
- Kabat-Zinn, J. (2013) *Full Catastrophe Living,.* New York, NY: Bantam Books.
- Lubbers, I. (2015, November 7). *The Scientific Benefits of Meditation-Science of People.* {Web log post]. Retrieved from http://www.scienceofpeople.com/2015/11/the-scientific-benefits-of-meditation/

- Melnick, M. (2013, May 2). *Meditation Health Benefits: What The Practice Does to Your Body.* [Web log post]. Retrieved from http://www.huffingtonpost.com/2013/04/30/meditation-health-benefits_n_3178731.html
- OnlineMBA.com Staff Writer. (n.d.) *10 Companies That Promote Employee Meditation.* [Web log post]. Retrieved from http://www.onlinemba.com/blog/10-big-companies-that-promote-employee-meditation/
- Radcliff, N. (2017, January 6). *Health Benefits of Meditation- Washington Times.* [Web log post]. Retrieved from http://www.washingtontimes.com/news/2017/jan/6/health-benefits-meditation/

ASK FOR EDUCATION

Chapter 21: Intelligence and Achievement
- Balter, M. (2011, April 25). *What Does IQ Really Measure?* [Web log post]. Retrieved from http://www.sciencemag.org/news/2011/04/what-does-iq-really-measure
- Schneider, W. J. (2014, February 6). *History of Intelligence Theories: William Stern (1871-1938) The Individual Behind the Intelligence Quotient.* [Web log post]. Retrieved from

https://assessingpsyche.wordpress.com/2014/02/06/william-stern-1871-1938-the-individual-behind-the-intelligence-quotient/
- Theory of Multiple Intelligence. (n.d.) *Wikipedia.* Retrieved from https://en.wikipedia.org/wiki/Theory_of_multiple_intelligences
- University of New Hampshire Staff Writer. (n.d.) *What is Emotional Intelligence (EI).* [Web log post]. Retrieved from http://www.unh.edu/emotional_intelligence/ei%20What%20is%20EI/ei%20definition.htm

Chapter 22: Increasing Intelligence and How Learning Can Change the Brain

- Associated Press Staff Writer. (2005, March 5). *Yale Psychologist Designs Test: A Challenge to the SAT.* [Web log post]. Retrieved from http://usatoday30.usatoday.com/news/education/2005-03-05-sat-rainbow_x.htm
- Coyle, D. *The Talent Code: Greatness Isn't Born. It's Grown.* (2010). London, England: Arrow Books Ltd.
- Ely, P. (2015, May 22). *5 Ways to Increase your IQ(Because It's Not Set in Genetic Stone).* [Web log post]. Retrieved from

- http://www.success.com/blog/5-smart-ways-to-increase-your-iq-because-its-not-set-in-genetic-stone
- Kohler, C. (2009, September 1). *How Tetris Changes Your Brain-Wired Magazine.* [Web log post]. Retrieved from https://www.wired.com/2009/09/how-tetris-changes-your-brain/
- Medina, J. (2014). *Brain Rules.* Seattle, WA: Pear Press.

Chapter 23: Mindset
- Bates-Grigsby, K. (2010, March 9). *Students Stand and Deliver for Former Teacher.* [Web log post]. Retrieved from http://www.npr.org/templates/story/story.php?storyId=124491340
- Dweck, C. (2006). *Mindset.* New York, NY: Ballantine Books.
- History Hollywood Staff Writer. (n.d.) *McFarland USA vs. The True Story of Coach White's 1987 Team.* [Web log post]. Retrieved from http://www.historyvshollywood.com/reelfaces/mcfarland-usa/
- Tucker, R. (2014, May 11). *The Wacky but True Story Behind 'Million Dollar Arm.'* [Web log post]. Retrieved from http://nypost.com/2014/05/11/the-wacky-but-true-story-behind-million-dollar-arm/

Chapter 24: Deep Practice

- Barr, C. (n.d.) *Deliberate Practice: What It Is and Why You Need It.*. [Web log post]. Retrieved from http://expertenough.com/1423/deliberate-practice
- Coyle, D. *The Talent Code: Greatness Isn't Born. It's Grown.* (2010). London, England: Arrow Books Ltd.
- Ericsson, K. A. & Pool, R. Peak. (2017). *Peak: Secrets from the New Science of Expertise.* New York, NY: Houghton Mifflin Harcourt.
- Knutson-Bueling, R. (2010, February 18). *The Creation of an Olympic Figure Skater.* [Web log post]. Retrieved from http://acsmolympics.typepad.com/acsm-winter-olympics-expert-commentary/2010/02/the-creation-of-an-olympic-figure-skater.html

Chapter 25: Coaching

- Lefevre, G. (n.d.) *High School Coach Imposes Own Basketball Lockout.* [Web log post]. Retrieved from http://www.cnn.com/US/9901/07/team.lockout/index.html?eref=sitesearch
- Patterson, S. (2005). *From Lockout to Open Doors: George Fox.* [Web log post]. Retrieved from http://www.georgefox.edu/journalonline/winter05/lockout.html
- Tom House. (n.d.) *Wikipedia.* Retrieved from https://en.wikipedia.org/wiki/Tom_House

- Yaeger, D. (2016, November 2). *John Wooden's Legacy Is a How-to Guide for A Successful Life.* [Web log post]. Retrieved from http://www.success.com/article/john-woodens-legacy-is-a-how-to-guide-for-a-successful-life

ASK FOR SUCCESS

Chapter 26: The Meaning of Success
- Egan, M. (2015, July 24). *Ex-NBA Star Went from $108 Million to Bankruptcy.* [Web log post]. Retrieved from http://money.cnn.com/2015/07/24/investing/antoine-walker-nba-bankruptcy/
- The Family Man. (n.d.) *Wikipedia.* Retrieved from https://en.wikipedia.org/wiki/The_Family_Man

Chapter 27: Why We Fail
- Corley, T. *Rich Habits - The Daily Success Habits of Wealthy Individuals.* Minneapolis, MN: Langdon Street Press.

Chapter 28: Attract Success Into Your Life
- BBC Staff Writer. (2014, January 3). *Natan Sharansky: How Chess Kept One Man Sane.* [Web log

post]. Retrieved from
http://www.bbc.com/news/magazine-25560162
- Haefner, J. (n.d.) *Visualization: The Secret to Improving Your Game Without Touching a Basketball.* [Web log post]. Retrieved from https://www.breakthroughbasketball.com/mental/visualization.html

Chapter 29: Regrets: What Gets Left Behind
- Ware, B. (2012). *The Top 5 Regrets of the Dying.* Carlsbad, CA: Hay House.

Chapter 30: Gratitude
- Emmons, R. C. *Thanks!: How the New Science of Gratitude Can Make You Happier.* (2007). New York, NY: Houghton Mifflin Harcourt.

ABOUT THE AUTHOR

Richard Bellman assists leaders and entrepreneurs with leadership training, motivational seminars and life and business coaching. Richard's unique and extensive experience in training, leadership, and coaching, provides for a unique and transformative experience for his clients.

For the past 30 years, Richard has acted in the service of others through his varied classes and presentations. Throughout his career he has taught adults a wide range of subjects such as ESL; Food Safety; Security Guard Training; Pesticide Applicator Training and business skills.

Currently he trains for one of the largest seminar companies in the United States and travels throughout the country lecturing and training individuals and business leaders on leadership, management and communication skills. He currently conducts life coaching with individuals and business leaders who want to get more out of their personal and business life. For more information or to inquire about Richard's availability, please call (310) 684-8241 or visit his website at:

http://richardbellmanspeaks.com/

www.ingramcontent.com/pod-product-compliance
Lightning Source LLC
Chambersburg PA
CBHW071654160426
43195CB00012B/1468